THE CANTICLES OF THE LITURGICAL HOURS

THE CANTICLES OF THE LITURGICAL HOURS

Praise from the Ends of the Earth

GREGORY J. POLAN, OSB

Paulist Press
New York / Mahwah, NJ

Cover image, "Christ the Word," by Father Rubeval Monteiero da Silva, OSB, professor of art and architecture at the Pontifical Faculty of Liturgy at Sant'Anselmo in Rome
Cover and book design by Lynn Else

Library of Congress Cataloging-in-Publication Data
Names: Polan, Gregory J., 1950– author
Title: The canticles of the Liturgical hours: praise from the ends of the Earth / Gregory J. Polan.
Description: New York: Paulist Press, [2025] | Summary: "This work is an exegetical and spiritual commentary on the Canticles of the Liturgy of the Hours for Lauds and Vespers"—Provided by publisher.
Identifiers: LCCN 2024051557 (print) | LCCN 2024051558 (ebook) | ISBN 9780809157563 paperback | ISBN 9780809189236 ebook
Subjects: LCSH: Catholic Church. Liturgy of the hours | Divine office
Classification: LCC BX2000 .P65 2025 (print) | LCC BX2000 (ebook) | DDC 264/.02015—dc23/eng/20250402
LC record available at https://lccn.loc.gov/2024051557
LC ebook record available at https://lccn.loc.gov/2024051558

ISBN 978-0-8091-5756-3 (paperback)
ISBN 978-0-8091-8923-6 (ebook)

Published by Paulist Press
997 Macarthur Boulevard
Mahwah, NJ 07430
www.paulistpress.com

Printed and bound in the
United States of America

CONTENTS

Preface ix

Part I: Canticles for Morning Prayer 1

Week 1 3

Sunday—Daniel 3:57–88, 56 3

Monday—1 Chronicles 29:10–13 7

Tuesday—Tobit 13:1b–8 10

Wednesday—Judith 16:1–2, 13–15 14

Thursday—Jeremiah 31:10–14 17

Friday—Isaiah 45:15–25 20

Saturday—Exodus 15:1–4a, 8–13, 17–18 24

Week 2 29

Sunday—Daniel 3:52–57 29

Monday—Sirach 36:1–7, 13, 16–19 32

Tuesday—Isaiah 38:10–14a, 17–20 35

Wednesday—1 Samuel 2:1–10 39

Thursday—Isaiah 12:1–6 42

Friday—Habakkuk 3:2–4, 13a, 15–19 46

Saturday—Deuteronomy 32:1–12 50

Week 3 55
Sunday—Daniel 3:57–88, 56 55
Monday—Isaiah 2:2–5 58
Tuesday—Isaiah 26:1b–4, 7–9, 12 62
Wednesday—Isaiah 33:13–16 66
Thursday—Isaiah 40:10–17 68
Friday—Jeremiah 14:17–21 72
Saturday—Wisdom 9:1–6, 9–11 76

Week 4 80
Sunday—Daniel 3:52–57 80
Monday—Isaiah 42:10–16 83
Tuesday—Daniel 3:26–27, 29, 34–41 87
Wednesday—Isaiah 61:10–11; 62:1–5 91
Thursday—Isaiah 66:10–14a 96
Friday—Tobit 13:1b–6 100
Saturday—Ezekiel 36:24–28 104

Part II: Canticles for Evening Prayer 109
Sunday 1 / Saturday Evening—Philippians 2:6–11 111
Sunday 2—Revelation 19:1–2, 5–7 116
Monday—Ephesians 1:3–10 118
Tuesday—Revelation 4:11; 5:9b–10, 12b 122
Wednesday—Colossians 1:12–20 125
Thursday—Revelation 11:17–18; 12:10b–12a 129
Friday—Revelation 15:3–4 131

Seasonal Canticles 135
Epiphany—1 Timothy 3:16 135
Sundays in Lent—1 Peter 2:21–24 138

Part III: Gospel Canticles 143
Canticle of Mary (Luke 1:46–55) 145
Canticle of Zechariah (Luke 1:68–79) 149
Canticle of Simeon (Luke 2:29–32) 153

PREFACE

IN THE FIFTY-THREE years of my life as a Benedictine monk, the daily celebration of the Liturgy of the Hours has been a constant source of life-giving strength and meaning. The daily celebrations of the Eucharist and the Liturgy of the Hours—widely referred to as the Divine Office—are the rhythmic pulses that sustain monastic life. A natural intensity emerges as the familiar psalms and canticles are sung or recited and heard over and over again, week after week and year after year. At the same time, our awareness that the word of God is truly present in these sacred texts calls us who pray them each day to a new and generative response to the divine voice as it emerges from them. The daily practice of *Lectio Divina*—the spiritual exercise of meditative reading of the sacred texts—opens the human heart more and more fully to the presence and power that is in the word of God. This divine impulse invites us to hear the voice of God speaking in ways that can both touch our individual lives and affect the movement of the whole world. The words of Scripture we encounter in the Eucharist and the Liturgy of the Hours work to transform the human heart, leading it onward in our search for God, which occupies us always and everywhere.

This is not to say, of course, that the prayer of the Liturgy of the Hours is the exclusive domain of monks. We need only consider the teaching of the Second Vatican Council to recognize that this is not remotely the case. In *Sacrosanctum Concilium*, the Constitution on the Sacred Liturgy, the Council affirms that the recitation of the Liturgy of the Hours is indeed the prayer of the *whole* Church:

> The divine office, because it is the public prayer of the Church, is a source of piety, and nourishment for personal prayer. And therefore priests and all others who take part in the divine office are earnestly exhorted in the Lord to attune their minds to their voices when praying it. The better to achieve this, let them take steps to improve their understanding of the liturgy and of the bible, especially of the psalms. (SC 90)

As "the public prayer of the Church," the Liturgy of the Hours belongs to all the faithful, the members of the Body of Christ. And it is especially to help "improve their understanding" of the texts used in the Liturgy of the Hours that this book is written.

The Liturgy of the Hours has for centuries included biblical texts in addition to the 150 songs of worship actually designated as the Book of Psalms. These passages, usually categorized as "canticles" (which means "little songs"), are interspersed among the psalms and prayed along with them. Specifically, they are included as the second sung text at the morning office of Lauds, the third text at the evening office of Vespers, and the gospel song that follows the response to the reading. These canticles are drawn from the writings of the prophets, from the Wisdom authors, and from other prayers found in the Old Testament. They are also taken from New Testament sources, such as the letters of Saint Paul and Saint Peter, and the Book of Revelation. They bear a likeness to psalms in that they are often emphatic expressions of prayer rendered in poetic form. But these selections include a variety of literary genres that are worthy of note. They sometimes express themes or images proper to the time of day at which they are recited, or to the season of the year—such as Advent, Lent, or

Easter—in which they are inserted into a particular hour of the office.

To my knowledge, little has been written specifically about these canticles. Yet they have long been a rich deposit of faith and an enduring source of inspiration; their presence in the Divine Office gives witness that from Old Testament times into the Christian era, they have been preserved for the use of the Church at prayer. They are inspired writings: God continues to speak to us through them, inviting us to respond to their many and varied invitations to follow in the way of holiness. It is my hope that this book will supplement the reader's understanding of the texts made available to us in the Liturgy of the Hours, and thus enhance our prayer.

I am grateful for the invitation of Paulist Press to compose for publication this series of brief commentaries and reflections on the canticles of the Liturgy of the Hours. This work would not have been completed without the considerable help of one of my confreres, Br. Jude Person, OSB, of Conception Abbey. His literary skills as a copy editor have made a world of difference for the smooth, consistent, reasoned, and articulate representation of the ideas presented. And finally, to my community at Conception Abbey, I express my deep gratitude for the opportunities for graduate study in Scripture and for my formation in the rich monastic tradition.

Abbot Gregory J. Polan, OSB
Abbot Primate of the Benedictine Confederation
Sant'Anselmo, Rome

I

CANTICLES FOR MORNING PRAYER

WEEK 1

SUNDAY

Daniel 3:57–88, 56

The Marvelous Works of the Lord

THE BOOK OF DANIEL appears in most Catholic Bibles as the fourth of the major prophets. However, in the Jewish tradition, this same book belongs to the last assemblage of biblical texts known as the "Writings," sometimes referred to as the Wisdom collection. This prayer of praise is used in the Roman Liturgy of the Hours at Morning Prayer on Sundays 1 and 3. A reader might ask, "Why can't I find this text in my Bible?" The answer is that some biblical texts—like this one—have come down to us only through the Greek translation of the Hebrew Bible known as the Septuagint. Nevertheless, these ancient writings have always been part of the Catholic canon of Scriptures. In translations based on the Hebrew Masoretic text, these biblical passages are often located in an appendix for the so-called deuterocanonical texts. "Deuterocanonical" means the "second canon" (Greek)—a collection that in the Catholic tradition completes the "first canon" (Hebrew)

The story behind this canticle tells of the three young Jewish men—Hananiah, Azariah, and Mishael—who were thrown into the fiery furnace by King Nebuchadnezzar of Babylon. Unwilling to serve the Babylonian god, they had refused to offer worship to a golden idol set up by the king (Dan 3:1–23). In the biblical text, this canticle is preceded by the song sometimes called the "Prayer of Azariah in the Furnace." His prayer praises the God of just deeds and right judgments, whose gracious forgiveness is bestowed upon those who have wandered from the divine commandments. The three-part conclusion of the full prayer includes, first, an acknowledgment of God as sole Lord, followed by a promise to follow God with their whole hearts, and finally a prayer for deliverance.

As the king's servants continue to stoke the fires of the furnace, God's angel comes down from heaven and drives away the flames, leaving the space as if a dewy breeze had refreshed it (Dan 3:50). Unharmed, the three young men raise their voices to bless and glorify God. Close attention to this litany of praise reveals an ordering of the elements of creation called to give glory to God. In vv. 57–61, the three young men bid those works of God that manifest divine sovereignty to offer their praise: the heavens, angelic powers, waters above and below the heavens. In vv. 62–73, they turn their call to those elements of creation that govern human existence, foster life, and mark the spans of time: sun and moon, stars of heaven, showers and dew, winds, fire and heat, cold and chill, the rains, frost and snow, night and day. In vv. 74–82, their words summon the praise of all that fills land and sea: all that grows, the waters that spring up from the earth, creatures inhabiting the waters, birds of the air, all the beasts. In vv. 83–88, the litany calls the whole human race to praise: first, the nation that is God's people, Israel; then those counted especially among God's servants, the just and humble of heart; and finally the three young men urge themselves to fullness of praise—Hananiah, Azariah, and Mishael, whose faith has brought them God's deliverance.

What a perfect canticle of praise this is for the Sunday celebration: Sunday, the first day of creation, and the day of our new creation through the saving death and resurrection of Christ. In a context of profound faith, these three young men, exiled to a foreign land, refuse to worship any but the one true God; their faith, conviction, and trust enable them to perceive the saving hand of God in their lives in a wondrous way. Sure that their faith is saving them, they look to the world around them; they offer thanks for the marvels of creation and the magnificent order in which God has fashioned it. In our own moments of darkness, doubt, and fear, we too need to stand firm in our faith. When we look at the world in which our daily lives are lived out, we recognize the God who fosters life within and around us, even when we do not feel that transforming power. Let our faith be strong that we too may experience God's saving love, as we await the transformation of our hearts and bodies to be in conformity with Christ's glorious life within us (Rom 8:35–36; Phil 3:20).

Daniel 3:57–88, 56

57 Bless the Lord, all you works of the Lord,
praise and highly exalt him forever.

58 Heavens, bless the Lord,
59 angels of the Lord, bless the Lord.
60 All waters above the heavens, bless the Lord,
61 all powers, bless the Lord.

62 Sun and moon, bless the Lord,
63 stars of heaven, bless the Lord.
64 Every shower and dew, bless the Lord,
65 all winds, bless the Lord.

66 Fire and heat, bless the Lord,
67 cold and heat, bless the Lord.
68 Dew and rain, bless the Lord,
69 frost and cold, bless the Lord.

70 Ice and snows, bless the Lord,
71 nights and days, bless the Lord.
72 Light and darkness, bless the Lord,
73 lightnings and clouds, bless the Lord.

74 Let the earth bless the Lord,
praise and highly exalt him forever.

75 Mountains and hills, bless the Lord,
76 all that grows on the earth, bless the Lord.
77 Seas and rivers, bless the Lord,
78 springs of water, bless the Lord.

79 Sea beasts and all that move in the water, bless the Lord,
80 all birds of heaven, bless the Lord.
81 All wild beasts and cattle, bless the Lord,
82 all you people, bless the Lord.

83 O Israel, bless the Lord,
praise and highly exalt him forever.

84 Priests of the Lord, bless the Lord,
85 servants of the Lord, bless the Lord.
86 Spirits and souls of the just, bless the Lord,
87 holy and humble of heart, bless the Lord.
88 Hananiah, Azariah, Mishael, bless the Lord,
praise and highly exalt him forever.

Let us bless the Father, and the Son, with the Holy Spirit.
Let us praise and highly exalt him forever.
56 Blessed are you in the firmament of heaven,
worthy of praise and highly exalted forever.

Canticle Prayer

O wondrous Creator of all that surrounds us, help us to see you in the daily movements of our lives, and help us to join creation's symphony of praise and thanksgiving for your saving acts of goodness, mercy, and deliverance. Through Christ, our risen Lord.

MONDAY

1 Chronicles 29:10–13

All Is Yours

To begin our reflection on this canticle, let's consider a tale taken from the sayings of the Desert Fathers about a man of zealous faith who wanted to discover the best way to live a life of true sanctity. He knew that the Desert Fathers in Egypt were renowned for holiness. "If I can speak with one of them," he said, "he will be able to answer my question immediately." So this man set out for the desert in search of a monastic Father widely known for wisdom and holiness. Upon finding one, he approached him, did him reverence, and politely posed his request: "Father, please tell me how I can become a saint." Sitting quietly, the monk closed his eyes in thought. After a few minutes, he opened his eyes, and gazing piercingly at the man, he said simply, "Hymns and doxologies." The man of zealous faith waited for further explanation, some clarification or elucidation or course of action, but the Father said nothing else. Twice more the man asked the monk the same question, but each time he received the same answer. The visit ended, and the man went home. For many days he pondered the monk's response, but its meaning became no clearer to his mind. "Well," he said finally, "I may not understand, but I can certainly do what he said." So he began to sing hymns and doxologies, simply as an exercise of his faith. And what began as a mere exercise soon became a true external expression of internal faith. Praise and thanksgiving offered to God had begun to change him. Having put the monk's words into practice, they finally began to make sense. The man of faith came to understand that sanctity in life comes to us by living the words of the Psalms, giving glory to God at all times. This principle is beautifully expressed in the opening verses of Psalm 34: "I will bless the LORD at all times; praise of him is always in my mouth."

The word *doxology* comes from the Greek *doxa* meaning "glory," and *logos* meaning "word." Doxology means the lifting up of words of praise and thanksgiving in an attitude of awe and wonder. To recite a doxology is to give glory and honor to God. The frequent appearance of doxologies in both Scriptures and worship was already a central element of the Jewish faith prior to the advent of Christianity; Psalms 41, 72, 89, and 106 conclude with a doxology, while all of Psalm 150 is considered a doxology for the whole Psalter. Christians continued this practice in their distinct formulations of praise for the Holy Trinity: "Glory to the Father and to the Son and to the Holy Spirit."

In this brief canticle from 1 Chronicles, King David addresses to God words of blessing and praise, honor and thanksgiving, acknowledging God's wondrous works both in the heavens and on the earth. He confesses who God is both in his life and in the wonders of creation that surround all people. This short doxology is intentionally inclusive, making use of the word *all* four times: "*all* is yours" (v. 11c), "exalted as head over *all*" (v. 11e), "you have dominion over *all*" (v. 12b), and "your hand gives greatness and strength to *all*" (v. 12d). It concludes with expressions of thanks and praise to God's splendid name (v. 13). (In the Scriptures, to speak of God's "name" in a context of agency is an idiomatic way of referring to God's deeds or actions.)

This canticle provides a beautiful introduction to this important mode of expression of faith in our own lives. Whether in our morning or evening prayers, or in the wider Church's praise of the marvelous deeds of the Trinity in our world today, or simply in moments of personal wonder at hearing God's voice in our own lives, doxology can give voice to moments of profound communion with God. In the Gospel of Luke, we find Jesus himself breaking forth in a spontaneous exclamation of doxology that bespeaks the intensity of his relationship with God: "At that very moment, [Jesus] rejoiced [in] the holy Spirit and said, 'I give you thanks, Father, Lord of heaven and earth, for although you have hidden these things from the wise and the learned, you have revealed them to the childlike'" (Luke 10:21). Our own doxological utterances can demonstrate in an essential way our personal relationship with God; such prayer reminds us of who God is in our life and who we are before God. If the wisdom of the Desert Father recounted earlier remains true in our own lives, our recitation of authentic expressions of praise and thanksgiving can indeed lead us on our way to holiness; they can deepen the relationship between us and God in new and profound expressions of faith.

1 Chronicles 29:10–13

10 Blessed are you, O Lord,
God of Israel, our father,
from eternity unto eternity.

11 Yours, O Lord, is greatness and power,
splendor, victory and majesty;
for all is yours in heaven and on earth.
Yours, O Lord, is the kingdom,
you are exalted as head over all.

12 Riches and honor are from you,
and you have dominion over all.

In your hand is power and might;
your hand gives greatness and strength to all.

13 And now, our God, we give you thanks,
and we praise your splendid name.

Canticle Prayer

Blest are you, God of mercy and compassion, who daily show us the ways of wisdom and insight. Help us to hear your voice and guide our hearts in praise of your holy name, you who live and reign forever and ever. Amen.

TUESDAY

Tobit 13:1b–8

Turn Back to God

The Book of Tobit is a unique book in the Bible. It tells the story of a righteous man living in exile with his family in the Assyrian city of Nineveh. The narrative treats themes of parental love, filial care for elders, young love veiled in mystery, and the overcoming of evil forces by the power of righteous living and divine protection. The text is pregnant with situations of waiting for blessing to become manifest. The righteous Tobit is bereft of blessing, as are his son Tobiah and Tobiah's fiancée Sarah. The intervention of God through the agency of an angel brings the story to a distinctive conclusion. The story also bears many traditional tropes and themes from all major sections of the Bible. First, the retribution motif of the Deuteronomic tradition figures strongly in Tobit; that is, good deeds and faith bring blessings, while violation of the law brings God's wrath (Deut 5:32–33; 28:1–2, 15; Tob 4:5–6). Second, the text recalls a moment recounted more fully in the historical books: the people of the northern kingdom being deported to live as captives in Assyria (2 Kgs 17—18; Tob 1:3). Third, Tobit echoes the depiction of family life as the model of righteous living presented in the Wisdom literature: from their own experience, parents give instruction to their children, thus forming a new generation in prudence and right judgment (Proverbs 1). Such educative proverbs and sayings recur throughout the text (Tob 4:3–11; 6:16; 12:6–10; 14:8–10). Fourth, motifs from the Psalms recur in the Book of Tobit in Prayers of Petition (Tob 3:2–6, 8:16–17) and Hymns of Thanksgiving (Tob 11:14–15; 13:1–18).

The story recounted in the Book of Tobit weaves its way through Tobit's experience of blindness (Tob 2:9–14) to the regaining of his sight (11:9–15), but does so by focusing on the encounter of his son Tobiah with the angel Raphael. Tobit commands his son to retrieve some money he has deposited in the distant city of Rages in Media. God sends the disguised angel Raphael (a name that means "God heals") to accompany the young Tobiah. In the midst of this journey, Tobiah meets a kinswoman named Sarah, who has borne the death of seven successive husbands, each on their wedding night, to the machinations of a demon. Tobiah marries her, but following Raphael's instruction he applies the entrails of a fish to hot embers, which drives away the demon. Tobiah's life and the marriage are preserved. After feasting with the family of Sarah and collecting his father's money, Tobiah, Sarah, and Raphael return to Nineveh. Again at the command of Raphael, Tobiah applies the gall of the fish to the eyes of his father Tobit, whose sight is restored. Upon recognition of this blessing, Tobit utters a long hymn of thanksgiving. A section of this hymn is chanted at Morning Prayer on Tuesday of Week One (Tob 13:2–8) and a second section on Friday of Week Four (Tob 13:8–11, 13–14ab, 15–16ab).

One sees the movement and experience of the paschal mystery in this canticle in a series of contrasting tribulations and blessings in human experience. Notice the shift in language describing the divine-human encounter: God leads down to the depths of

Hades and then brings up from ruin (v. 2); God punishes yet has mercy, having gathered again the scattered people (v. 4); "Turn back, you sinners, and do what is right," we are exhorted, for God may again show favor and mercy (v. 6ff.). God's mercy and grace are indeed eternal themes. In *The Name of God Is Mercy*, Pope Francis tells us that the Lord looks for only a "glimmer of space" where we admit wrongdoing and seek forgiveness. God will enter into that little space and open wide for us the doors of mercy, manifesting the infinite expanse of divine love, of mercy for the repentant sinner. The Psalmist reminds us, "As far as the east is from the west, so vast is the divine mercy that forgives our transgressions (Ps 103:12).

Saint Paul expresses the same idea, asserting that the one righteous act of Christ's paschal sacrifice has brought us divine mercy: "Just as through one transgression condemnation came upon all, so through one righteous act acquittal and life came to all. For just as through the disobedience of one person the many were made sinners, so through the obedience of one the many will be made righteous" (Rom 5:18–19). Each of us experiences Tobit's unique and beautiful hymn of thanksgiving as if we were the only one who could sing it; as each of us gathers up his or her uniquely personal encounters with sin, God takes them and transforms them by the mystery of divine grace into new life and new hope that overflows in gratitude for blessings beyond measure. Let our thanksgiving strive to meet the measure of God's mercy and faithfulness, with hearts full of praise for the wonders of divine love that each and every day are showered upon us.

Tobit 13:1b–8

1b Blessed be God, who lives forever,
and blessed be his kingdom,
2 for he punishes but also shows mercy.

He leads down to the depths of Hades,
and brings up from ruin by his majesty;
and no one can escape his hand.

3 Children of Israel, confess him before the nations,
for he has scattered you among them,
4 and even there has shown you his greatness.

Extol him, then, before every living being,
for he is our Lord and our Father,
he is our God forever.

5 He will punish you for your iniquities,
but on all of you he will have mercy,
he will gather you from all the nations
wherever you have been scattered.

6 When you turn back to him
with all your heart and all your soul
to do what is true before him,
then he will turn back to you
and no longer hide his face from you.

Now, then, see what he has done for you,
and with full voice, give him your thanks.
Bless the Lord of righteousness,
and exalt the King of the ages.

In the land of my exile I give him thanks,
and show his power and grandeur to a nation of
sinners.
Turn back, you sinners, and do what is right before him.
Who knows, he may favor you and show you mercy?

[7] To the King of heaven I speak joyfully,
my soul rejoices all the days of my life.
[8] Bless the Lord, all you chosen ones;
and all, give praise to his grandeur.
Take up days of rejoicing and confess him.

Canticle Prayer

God of love and mercy, who guide the course of human history, help us to recognize your gracious guidance in the movements of our lives. Let our response to your goodness always be ready praise and profound thanksgiving, through Christ our Lord. Amen.

WEDNESDAY

Judith 16:1–2,13–15

Tambourines and Cymbals

The context of this Canticle of Judith is that of a prayer of thanksgiving as a faithful and noble response to God for the divine assistance given to her and to the people of Israel. Amid a time of war and political uncertainty, Judith rises up like one of the Judges, calling the leaders of the land to faith, prayer, and confidence in God's providential care for them (8:1–27). The elders of the people hear the wisdom of her words and follow her instructions. Her prayer is beautifully expressed (9:1–14) and her heroic deeds deliver the people from the outside forces in a stunning victory. Israel hails and acclaims her wise strategy in battle and its successful outcome. In the context of that celebration, we have Judith's praise of God's mighty hand in delivering the people from their enemies. Her renown is said to have been remembered by the people for many years (16:21). In the early writings of the Church, both Saint Clement of Rome and Saint Jerome speak of the great virtue and wise counsel of Judith. For the feasts of the Virgin Mary, language and imagery are drawn from the Book of Judith for the antiphons and texts of Marian celebrations, seeing in Judith aspects of the life of Mary. An example is one of the antiphons for Morning Prayer from the Common of the Blessed Virgin Mary: "You are the glory of Jerusalem, the joy of Israel; you are the fairest honor of our race" (cf. Jdt 15:9). The story of Judith's faith, trust, and powerful prayer was seen as important enough to be included in the canon of the Catholic Scriptures at the Council of Trent.

Judith bears a strong resemblance to other Old Testament women of faith and strength: the judge, Deborah (Judg 4—5), and the queen, Esther (Esth 4C—5). They both redeem their people from oppression and danger. One can also see parallels between Judith and the Wise Woman of Proverbs 31. Both are resourceful, independent in their care for themselves and others, and an honor to their kin, and for Judith, to her deceased husband (Jdt 8). There is also Judith and Esther who show themselves faithful to God's covenant and fervent in prayer. Judith prays a lament following the traditional custom of lying prostrate with ashes on her head while lamenting (Jdt 9) and later leads the assembly in a hymn of gratitude for God's deliverance through her (Jdt 14). Similarly, Esther pleads with God grieving over her situation, acknowledging her fidelity to God's law, and calling for divine assistance in this dire moment of potential national disaster (Esth 4C:12–40); and though victorious, no hymn of victory is attributed to her.

The Canticle of Judith suits the Office of Morning Prayer well. From beginning to end the words lift up praise to God for the abundance of divine assistance that has accompanied Judith and her companions. We can make her words our own. Her words echo images and language from the Psalms. The expression, to improvise a "new song" recurs several times in the Psalter (Pss 33:3; 96:1; 98:1; 149:1); this saying calls forth a look from deep within a person to acknowledge how God has acted in profound ways in one's life. The expression, "May all your creatures serve you," finds a parallel expression in Psalm 145 (Ps 145:4–7, 11–12, 19–21). To serve God and neighbor should be our joy. And the reference to God's creative act, "you spoke, and they were made" (cf. Ps 33:6, 9), and also, "You sent forth your Spirit, and they were created," repeats the text in Psalm 104 (Ps 104:30). God is forever recreating us by acts of faithful and divine love. All these parallels between Judith and the Psalms bespeak the providential and loving act of deliverance accomplished by God for his people. Though Judith leads her people to victory, she attributed the success to God's mighty hand (Jdt 16:5). This is why Saint Paul goes to such an extreme, repeating, "Let the one who would boast, boast in the Lord" (1 Cor 1:31; 3:21–23; 2 Cor 1:12; 10:17; Gal 6:14). It is God who acts mighty in the lives of each person, bringing salvation and redemption. As we seriously look into our lives, we can daily see the acts of God by which we are blessed, given gifts beyond measure, and cared for in a loving way. Each day provides an original and fresh way to "sing a new song" to the God of our salvation, delivering us from the bonds of our personal slavery to self and to our world, and offering us a path to peace and glory in Christ Jesus our Lord.

Judith 16:1–2, 13–15

[1] Begin a song to my God with tambourines;
sing to my Lord with cymbals.
Improvise a new song for him;
extol and invoke his name.

[2] You are God who suppresses wars,
who pitches camp in the midst of your people
to free me from the hands of my pursuers.

13 I will sing a new song to my God:
O Lord, you are great and glorious,
marvelous in strength and invincible.

14 May all your creatures serve you,
for you spoke, and they were made.
You sent forth your Spirit, and they were created;
and no one can resist your voice.

15 For the mountains shall be shaken to their bases
like the waters;
rocks shall melt like wax before your face.
Yet to those who fear you, you will still show mercy.

Canticle Prayer

God of power and might, mercy and compassion, enable us to see your loving hand in the movement of events in our times. Even in the moments of disappointment and challenge, help us to remain strong in faith, trusting in your providential care. Through Christ our Lord.

THURSDAY

Jeremiah 31:10–14

The Grain, the Wine, and the Oil

The prophecy of Jeremiah brings to mind a book containing a long series of laments and judgments. Yet in the very heart of the book, in chapters 30–33, there is a collection of oracles that tell of the reestablishment and rebuilding of Jerusalem, and the renewal and restoration of the people of Israel and Judah. Amid all the laments, some have called it "a little book of consolation and comfort," not unlike what is found in Isaiah 40—55. Yet, these oracles carry a distinctly Jeremiah-like flavor in their language and imagery. Jeremiah preaches the true message of crisis brought about by the sins of the people; yet this interlude of hope prophecies a rebirth of the nation to be lived with God's law deeply embedded in the hearts of the people. Like a mantra that repeats itself through these chapters, the prophet restates several times the promise of God, "I will restore their fortunes [in the land of Judah]" (Jer 31:23; 32:44; 33:7, 11, 26). Though Jeremiah was a prophet to the southern kingdom of Judah, his prophesies of restoration also include the northern kingdom of Israel, which had been taken captive by Assyria. For both nations, through the prophet, God promises a healing that will enable the people to see both how they have squandered God's covenant, and how that covenant can be renewed with the hope it offers them. Herein lies the message of Jeremiah 31:1–14.

The opening words that speak about "gathering the scattered" are significant for understanding this canticle. God's covenant served to be a unifying element of the people; we are told that they were once a people of "mixed ancestry" (Exod 12:38) as they left Egypt. But in the offering of the covenant and their acceptance of obedience to the law, they sealed the covenant relationship and became a kingdom of priests and a holy people (Exod 19:6). God's covenant would unite them into the one people of God. God's gathering of these people is an eschatological sign of the covenant's promise: "I will be their God, and they shall be my people" (Exod 6:7; Lev 26:12; Deut 26:18). Being taken off into exile by both the Assyrians and Babylonians, the people who were once united on the God-given land were now scattered and living among foreigners. God's loving act of "gathering" them together renews the covenant that had been broken by their disregard for the law. As the canticle continues, it enumerates the blessings of God's renewed care for them. The "bread (grain harvested in spring), the wine (grapes harvested in summer) and the oil (olives harvested in autumn)" represent the three seasons of agricultural growth, a full year of divine providence. This and the other images of flocks and herds represent signs of abundance. It culminates with the vision of the inner soul of the people that will be likened to a watered garden—fresh and life-giving. The closing strophe that names the full recipients of God's blessings—young and old, mourning and consoled—will experience God's bounty.

One of the elements of this canticle that is often missed is that is contains a commission: "Declare this word to the nations and distant coasts" (Jer 31:10). The liberation and deliverance that is given by God must be made known to others. It is God's redemption that has taken place; Jacob has been ransomed from a hand too strong and powerful for him. God's work of redemption exceeds human expectation. Now the recipients of this covenantal gift must make it known to the world, to the far-off shores. In the New Testament, the First Letter of Peter echoes this text, relating it to the victory of God in Christ Jesus, offering us the new life that flows from his resurrection. There we read, "You are a chosen race, a royal priesthood, a holy nation, a people of his own, so that you may announce the praises of him who called you out of darkness into his wonderful light. Once you were 'no people,' but now you are God's people; you 'had not received mercy' but now you have received mercy" (1 Pet 2:9–10). God continues to renew the final covenant made through the saving and redemptive blood of Christ. It is our commission to proclaim this in word, and especially in deed. Knowing the price of our redemption impels us to be ambassadors of God's covenant of gracious love and unending mercy.

Jeremiah 31:10–14

10 Hear the word of the LORD, O nations;
declare it to the distant isles and say,
"He who scattered Israel will gather him
and guard him as a shepherd his flock."

11 For the LORD has ransomed Jacob,
redeemed him from a hand too strong for him.

12 They shall come and sing praise on the heights of
Zion,
come streaming to the bounty of the Lord—
to the grain and the wine and the oil,
to the yearlings of the flock and the herd.
Their soul shall be like a watered garden,
and they shall languish no more.

13 Then the maiden shall rejoice in a dance,
the young men and old together.
"I will change their mourning into joy;
I will console them, giving gladness for sorrow.
14 I will fill with rich fare the souls of my priests,
and my people shall be filled with my bounty."

Canticle Prayer

Almighty God, who bestowed the covenant and the law upon your holy people, you continue to gather them into one consecrated people and commission them to be the ambassadors of your love and mercy. Open our hearts to hear your call and grant us the strength to fulfill your will in our own day and age. Through Christ our Lord.

FRIDAY

Isaiah 45:15–25

Hidden Yet Present

This canticle begins with a surprising expression of faith. In strong language, the prophet addresses God as the "hidden one":

"Truly you are a God who hides yourself." Why this manner of address to God? Earlier in this chapter, God calls King Cyrus "his anointed," and earlier, "my shepherd" (Isa 44:28). Cyrus was a pagan and foreign ruler; yet through his command, the exiles of Judah are freed to return to their homeland. Could it be that God used an unexpected and unpredicted instrument for the liberation of his people? Indeed, such divine actions explain why God's ways are hidden, mysterious, and even startling for the believer. The God of Jacob is Savior and Creator, doing what is just and upright, and bringing life from chaos; this is in contrast to the idols, the work of human hands, that fashion objects that can do nothing.

The language of the second half of this canticle paints a courtroom scene. The witnesses are told, "come, gather together, draw near, speak up, present your case." Unafraid to face any work of human design, God has shown readiness to respond to any request, any need of those who are faithful. The righteous Savior of Jacob stands as judge over the wooden idols who present themselves as gods, yet are unable to bring about salvation. Those who would pray to such gods lack the knowledge to know the impotence of any god other than the God and Savior of Israel. In bold and unflinching language, God attests that there is no other god but the righteous Savior of Israel. All the ends of the earth are instructed to turn to God, to find salvation therein, for there alone are righteousness and divine strength. The "universalism" spoken of in these chapters of Isaiah demonstrates that belonging to God's covenant demands full participation in the expectations of law, which honor the Lord as the one, true, and only God of the universe. Those who fail to do so will be brought to shame for their ignorance and arrogance. The prophet who initially spoke of God who remains hidden now manifests the glory, might, and power that belong to him who is the Creator of all people and all things. God's word never returns empty but fulfills what has been promised (45:23a; 55:10–11).

We can rightly ask ourselves, what is idolatry today in our world? In a wide-ranging sense, even from what we read in the Old Testament, idolatry puts anyone or anything above the love, respect, obedience, belief in, or worship that should alone be given to God. The Letter to the Colossians says it strongly: "If then you have been raised up with Christ, seek after those things that are above where Christ is, seated at the right hand of God" (translation mine). The emphasis on "where Christ is," gives direction to our values. Throughout the Gospel, Jesus shows us by his deeds what he valued most: an intimate relationship with the One whom he called *Abba*. That single-minded focus of his heart made it clear the meaninglessness of the accumulation of wealth and possessions, the need for prestige, self-absorption, seeking influence, and being in control. That short and simple sentence drawn from the Sermon on the Mount helps us to examine ourselves to see where the pockets of idolatry lie in our lives. "Where your treasure lies, there can your heart also be found" (Matt 6:21). For all of us, there are elements of idolatry in our lives, places where God's design for us disappears and fades from our view and self-understanding. Yet, as we see in the example of Jesus, everyone who wanders from the way has a ready and warm welcome back (Luke 15:22–32).

Isaiah 45:15–25

15 Truly you are a God who hides yourself,
O God of Israel, the Savior.
16 All of them are shamed and disgraced;
the makers of idols leave together in disgrace.

17 Israel is saved by the LORD with everlasting salvation.
You shall not be put to shame or disgrace for all eternity.

18 For thus says the LORD, Creator of the heavens,
God himself, who formed the earth and made it firm;

not as chaos did he create it;
but formed it to be lived in:
I am the LORD, and there is no other.

19 I did not speak in secret,
in a land of darkness;
I did not say to the descendants of Jacob,
"Seek me in vain."
I the LORD speak what is just,
I declare what is upright.

20 Gather together, and come;
draw near together, you survivors of the nations;
they have no knowledge, who lift up wooden idols,
and pray to a god who cannot save.

21 Speak up and present your case;
let them take counsel together.
Who has revealed this from long ago,
foretold it of old?

Was it not I, the LORD?
There is no other god but me,
a righteous God and a Savior—
there is none except me.

22 Turn to me and be saved,
all the ends of the earth.
For I am God and there is no other.

23 By my own self I swear it,
from my mouth has righteousness gone forth,
a word that shall not return.
For to me every knee shall bow,
and every tongue shall swear an oath.

[24] They will say to me, "Only in the LORD
are righteousness and strength;
all who were angry against him
shall come to him and be ashamed.
[25] In the LORD all the offspring of Israel
shall be justified and exult."

Canticle Prayer

O God of might and power, who reveal yourself in mystery and hiddenness, open our eyes to the daily wonders that surround us, that we may see You who guide us in the ways of justice, peace, and mercy. Through Christ Our Lord.

SATURDAY

Exodus 15:1–4a, 8–13, 17–18

Lord, Majestic in Holiness

This canticle stands out among others. It is the first hymn in the Bible. The Hebrew slaves, soon to become the people of God in a covenant relationship (see Exod 19—20), proclaim God's unimaginable and incredible deed on their behalf. By God's act of deliverance from the slavery of Egypt and now at the waters of the Sea of Reeds, the people respond with a song of praise to the One who has again liberated them. When the Egyptian leaders realize that they have released their workforce, they set out in hot pursuit to bring them back. Moses calls his fellow Hebrew slaves to confidence that God will act. "The LORD will fight for you; you have only to keep still" (Exod 14:14). Following the words of Moses, God provides for them. This single verse is strategic for understanding all that will follow, both in this hymn and in the developing story. Moses is God's servant and mediator, but most importantly, the LORD is the key actor who choreographs the events that show the power, might, strength, and will of the One, time and again, bringing release and freedom for this motley group of Hebrew slaves. This early acclamation of praise speaks of God as a warrior (Exod 15:3), who fights on behalf of those called to be "a kingdom of priests and a holy nation" (Exod 19:5b), God's own treasured possession. It is in seeing how God has fought for them that the people grow in faith and place their trust in the God of Abraham, Isaac, and Jacob.

A passing reference is made to "gods" (v. 11a), but the movement of this hymn focuses on the power of the God of the Hebrews. Three times the divine name YHWH (LORD) appears, giving witness to this early acclamation of faith. This great God of all creation is referred to in very personal terms: my strength and might, my salvation, my God, my father's God. This same manner of expression is found often in the Psalter, where God is referred to as "my light and my salvation" (cf. Ps 27:1; see also Pss 18:1–3; 144:2). Israel experienced a considerable closeness to God in this act of divine deliverance; the event of the exodus would happen again, and there would be many times when they would see the mighty hand of God once demonstrated to Pharaoh, and later to the leaders of the nations of Assyria and Babylon. Among the people of the Ancient Near East, there was the belief in a pantheon of gods who ruled the movements of creation and history. Here, Israel expresses its strong belief in this moment of divine authority and dominion. "Who is like you among the gods, O LORD? Who is like you, majestic in holiness, awesome in splendor, working wonders?" (v. 11). The God of Israel is the One and only God of true and lasting deliverance and power over all other forces.

The imagery used in this canticle brings to mind the opening chapter of the Book of Genesis, the creation story. The strong wind sweeping over the chaotic waters are elements that repeat themselves here in the epic story of the crossing of the Sea of Reeds, here told in poetic form. "The waters gathered; the waves stood like a wall; the deeps congealed" (Exod 15:8). "You blew with your breath, the sea covered them, they sank like lead in the mighty waters" (Exod 15:10). Could it be that the sacred author is trying to draw lines of connection between the creation story and the crossing of the Sea of Reeds? Certainly the canticle uses images similar to those in Genesis 1 to suggest that the divine action is a kind of new beginning, or even the creation of a people, saved by God's intervention. This canticle has an important place in the Paschal Vigil as the response to the story of the Sea of Reeds; the Church has interpreted this story as a prefiguring of the waters of baptism. As a whole, the canticle is a response of faith, praise, and thanksgiving to the God who has freed the Hebrews from slavery and led them on the road to freedom, as God's chosen people. We can add our voices to this first of hymns in the Bible, bringing our expressions of gratitude and acclamation to God's wondrous acts in the unfolding of human history, in the life of the Church, and in the lives of each of us.

Exodus 15:1–4a, 8–13, 17–18

[1] Let us sing to the LORD who has gloriously
triumphed;
horse and rider he has hurled into the sea.

[2] The LORD is my strength and might;
he has become my salvation.
This is my God, and I will praise him,
my father's God, and I will exalt him.

[3] The LORD is a warrior; the LORD is his name.
[4] The chariots of Pharaoh and his army
he has cast into the sea.

8 At the blast of your anger, the waters gathered;
the waves stood up like a wall;
the deeps congealed in the heart of the sea.

9 The foe said, "I will pursue, will overtake;
I will divide the spoil,
my soul shall have its fill of them.
I will bare my sword;
my hand shall destroy them."

10 You blew with your breath, the sea covered them;
they sank like lead in the mighty waters.
11 Who is like you among the gods, O LORD?

Who is like you, majestic in holiness,
awesome in splendor, working wonders?
12 You stretched out your right hand,
the earth swallowed them.

13 In your faithful love you guided the people you
redeemed.
In your strength you led them to your holy dwelling.

17 You will bring them in and plant them
upon the mount of your inheritance:
the place which you, O LORD, have made your
dwelling,
the holy place, O LORD, that your hands have
established.

18 The LORD will reign forever and ever.

Canticle Prayer

God of Creation and Lord of the Universe, though you govern all you have made, it is your people whom you continue to deliver and redeem. Renew in us the dignity of our baptismal calling and strengthen us to live it with generosity, faith, and mutual respect. Through Christ our Lord.

WEEK 2

SUNDAY

Daniel 3:52–57

Praised and Exalted Forever

THIS CANTICLE COMPRISES the six verses that immediately precede the verses from the same chapter of the Book of Daniel that make up the canticle for Sunday Week 1 (Dan 3:57–88, 56). You may recall that those verses take us through a list of God's creatures in an ordered and systematic way, voicing praise for the One who brought them into being. This Sunday the text is considerably shorter, and focuses not on creation but on Creator—the God of might and majesty who brings creation into being. How fitting it is that such direct praise of God should initiate this long canticle. It is proclaimed in its entirety over two sequential Sundays and calls to mind the first of days, the Sunday on which creation itself commenced at the command of the Creator, as is set forth so imaginatively and powerfully for us in the Book of Genesis. By referring to "the God of our ancestors" at the very beginning, this canticle of praise takes us back to the earliest history of the human race, when men and women first came to a recognition and realization of the God who has brought all into being, who stands above all created things, and whose might must be exalted forever.

Following the initial phrase that praises God directly, the text goes on, "Blessed is your glorious and holy name." In the biblical world, a person's "name" signifies his or her deepest identity. Recall the numerous times in Scripture when God changes the name of a person to signify a change in status, mission, or even personality—Abram becomes Abraham, Jacob becomes Israel, Sarai becomes Sarah. A prophet may bear a name that reveals a particular element of that prophet's character. Elijah, whose name means "My God is YHWH," finds himself in conflict with rulers who had chosen to worship and honor false gods. By his very name, the person of Elijah stands for the one and only God of Israel. Thus we see that in the Scriptures someone's name is often meant to show forth the very essence of that person.

This function of the name is especially important with reference to God. We know that throughout the Bible many names and titles are applied to God. When the text of our canticle praises God's "glorious and holy name" we note two words of particular significance. In the Bible, what is called "holy" is recognized as set apart, distinct from everything else, and truly awe-inspiring. When attributed to God, the designation bears a profound theological meaning. This God, marked by holiness and thus wholly apart, cares for and enters into relationship with the people he has created. The all-holy God has established a covenant with Israel, a covenant that distinguishes them from all other people. Thus to attribute "glory" to the name of God is to imply a divine greatness that exceeds the power of human comprehension. The Hebrew word for "glory" (*kavod*) literally means "heavy, weighty, powerful." The God of Israel is glorious in the redemptive and salvific work accomplished by the divine power and will. What is beyond human capacity, what transcends natural limitations, God accomplishes by manifesting divine glory. Thus the opening lines of this short canticle are substantial and solemn in giving expression to who God is, to how God acts, and to what God chooses to do in the realm of human experience.

Is it not truly significant that when Jesus taught his disciples to pray, he told them to say to God, "Hallowed be thy Name"? In other words, all that God is, all that God does, and all that God says to us sets apart the One whose name we know, the One to whom we pray. All that God does is rightly called holy because it is accomplished by what God is in essence—the Holy Name. The weight of these words of praise, given to us here in the Book of Daniel, encourages us to look deep into our lives and into the course of human events to see the hand of God at work. What we can only dream of and hope for in the course of human history, we transfer through our prayer into the hands of God. The lifting-up of our intentions becomes the sign of our solidarity with all of creation that "eagerly awaits the revelation" (Rom 8:19) of God's plan of salvation as it unfolds for all God's children, among whom we thankfully count ourselves.

Daniel 3:52–57

52 Blessed are you, O Lord, the God of our ancestors,
to be praised and highly exalted forever.

Blessed is your glorious and holy name,
to be highly praised and exalted forever.

53 Blessed are you in the temple of your holy glory,
to be highly praised and glorified forever.

54 Blessed are you on the throne of your kingdom,
to be praised and highly exalted forever.

55 Blessed are you who look into the depths,
seated upon the cherubim,
to be praised and highly exalted forever.

56 Blessed are you in the firmament of heaven,
worthy of praise and highly exalted forever.

57 Bless the Lord, all you works of the Lord,
praise and highly exalt him forever.

Canticle Prayer

God of wonder and majesty, who display your greatness in the daily rhythmic unfolding of light and dark, cold and heat, land and sky: hear our prayer and grant us the inspiration to know your presence in all creation, especially in each person created in your holy image. To you be all glory and praise, now and forever.

MONDAY

Sirach 36:1–7, 13, 16–19

Grant New Signs

When we encounter a text from the Book of Sirach, we automatically expect to find collections of brief wisdom sayings and succinct proverbs. Yet the Book of Sirach also presents a number of beautiful prayers, some of which have been placed among the canticles of the Liturgy of the Hours. The text before us is one of these. Though the chapter offers a considerably longer prayer, two sections of the text have been excised to create a single canticle. The biblical authors of prayers often describe God according to a particular situation—their need for assistance or their desire to offer praise and thanks. Here the author describes God as the One who is great in power and might, yet also inclined to kindness and prompt to manifest mercy. The canticle begins with a unique expression, calling to the "God of all." Thus we discover in this prayer an outlook that extends beyond an insular view of the chosen people of Israel to include foreign nations as well (v. 3). Though the author prays especially for Israel and the holy city of Jerusalem, a plea is voiced that divine power also be shown to the nations that do not yet know God, in the hope that they too may come to a knowledge of the One who works signs and wonders.

The power and might ascribed to the saving Lord of Israel sets their God apart from the pagan deities of the ancient Near East. As Creator of all peoples and all things, the God of Israel manifests greatness by altering the course of world events. Though among the smallest of nations and humbled by powerful peoples, Israel knows God's might through their numerous experiences of the Lord's saving redemption. The present prayer exhorts God to do the same for the foreign nations, so that they too may experience and know firsthand the divine will to save, to bless, and to renew *all* peoples. In the events through which Israel is saved from Egypt, Babylon, and Persia, God has revealed to the world powers of that age a universal authority that must leave them astonished and dumbfounded. Israel prays that the nations will come to possess the wisdom to see what God has done and to acknowledge their God as the one true Lord and Creator of all.

To affirm the conviction that divine *desire* is the motive behind such saving acts, the sacred author emphasizes that *mercy* and *compassion* are the hallmarks of God's deeds of power. The prayer now under consideration begins (v. 1) and concludes (v. 14) with a plea for mercy. Any consideration of a history marked by God's acts of redemption must recognize and admit that it is because of their sinful and errant ways that Israel has experienced such gracious mercy. We note that the plea carries a sense of familial relationship with God: they acknowledge their status as a people themselves called by the very name of God and distinguished as God's firstborn. Such tender language expresses a closeness to God based on firsthand experience of divine deliverance. For a nation that has been scattered through history among many foreign lands, the plea that they be gathered together once again further expresses the hope that what God has done before God will do again, now: gather them together, restore and take pity on them. These acts of kindness culminate when the place of God's presence in Zion is filled with majesty and glory.

This same sense of a universal call to share in the fullness of God's life is found in Saint Paul's letter to the Ephesians, where we read, "Now in Christ Jesus you who once were far off have become near by the blood of Christ" (2:13). This text of Saint Paul echoes an earlier verse in the Book of Isaiah: "Peace! Peace to those who are far and near" (57:19). We can see how God's call to share in redemption has continued through the centuries; it manifests the unfolding plan of God by which all will come to know the saving power of divine love—a universal call to salvation. Living in a world divided by war, discrimination, prejudice, racism, and civil strife, these words from the Book of Sirach encourage us to pray that divine mercy will bring us healing, hope, and a vision of God's wondrous purpose of unity and peace.

Sirach 36:1–7, 13, 16–19

1 Have mercy on us, God of all,
look upon us,
and show us the light of your mercies;

2 and send your fear upon the nations
who have not sought you out,
that they may know there is no God but you,
and may recount your wondrous deeds.

3 Raise your hand over the foreign nations,
that they may see your power.
4 As you have used us to show them your holiness,
so now use them to show us your greatness.

5 Thus will they know as we have known
that there is no God but you, O Lord.

6 Grant new signs and accomplish further wonders,
7 make glorious your hand, confirm your right arm.

13 Gather together all the tribes of Jacob,
16 and restore to them their heritage
as it was from the beginning.

17 Have mercy on your people called by your name:
Israel, whom you likened to your first-born.
18 Take pity on your holy city:
Jerusalem, the place where you rest.
19 Fill Zion with your majesty,
and your temple with your glory.

Canticle Prayer

God of all, Creator and Redeemer, show new signs and work new wonders in our own day, that we may experience the greatness of your power and compassion, and thus work together for the building of a world forged in bonds of unity, peace, and mutual respect. Through Christ our Lord.

TUESDAY

Isaiah 38:10–14a, 17–20

Can the Dead Give You Praise, O Lord?

Some of the Old Testament canticles in the Liturgy of the Hours are given special places beyond the basic four-week cycle. This canticle from Isaiah appears on Tuesday of Week 2, but it is also used in two other special offices: on Holy Saturday at Morning Prayer, and for the Office of the Faithful Departed. The historical context that frames this canticle is the story of King Hezekiah of

Judah. Struggling with a life-threatening illness, Hezekiah turns to the prophet Isaiah to beg for divine intervention on his behalf. The prophet assures him that God will indeed intervene: Hezekiah will be granted another fifteen years of life, and the city of Jerusalem will be secured against the threat of the invading Assyrian army (Isa 38:4–6). The canticle follows the pattern found in the Psalms of Thanksgiving: a complaint arises from personal illness and difficulty, but the speaker moves on to an expression of hope in God and concludes with words of praise and thanksgiving for divine mediation. This same story is repeated with slight variations in 2 Kings 20:1–11, where Hezekiah pleads his case and calls on the prophet Isaiah to do the same before God, who promises divine healing and security.

The prayer maps out the relationship between God and Hezekiah in hyperbolic terms: God is likened to a lion that crushes the bones of his prey, while Hezekiah is no more than a fledgling swallow moaning before a menacing assailant. While these forceful descriptions may strike us as exaggerated, it is important to realize how illness can often raise a sense of being overcome by something beyond our control. Faced with serious illness or death, the mind may take paths that, while not purely rational, nonetheless present themselves as genuinely perilous. The image of God as a Divine Weaver who severs the last thread of life is a potent representation of the One who holds power of life and death (v. 12). At the time this prayer was composed, entry into Sheol was seen as the final journey into darkness at life's close, a descent into an underworld in which there was no hope of return. To be delivered from the prospect of such a gloomy and meaningless existence was a reason for thanksgiving; we can see in the text a progressive development, from withdrawal from human existence (vv. 10–11) to images of what death means to Hezekiah specifically (vv. 12–14), and to recovery and a sense of divine redemption (vv. 17–20).

Something that may strike us as strange or even comical is the way Hezekiah speaks of what the end of his life will mean to

God. In a clever turn of phrase, the king reminds God, "If I am dead in Sheol, then I cannot give you thanks." We find similar expressions in the Psalms (Pss 6:6; 30:10). In a sense, there is a fundamental truth to this statement, an irony that may make us smile. Created by God, our purpose in life is to offer praise and thanks to the One who brings us into being, sustains us, and challenges us to consider the profound meaning of God's love for us. However we seek to do this, in acts of worship or in the words and deeds of life, we confront a great mystery: how in the care of God our lives move through suffering and death into eternal life. In stories and prayers like Hezekiah's, we encounter another human being in his passage through suffering, his near-death experience, and his ultimate recovery. In both his suffering and recovery, he sees the hand of God at work; it is, for him and for us, an important encounter with wisdom and an intimate experience of God.

In the unfolding of the Gospel accounts of the life of Jesus, we see how he too passed through the mystery of suffering, so movingly recounted in scenes in the Garden of Gethsemani (Matt 26:36–46; Mark 14:32–42; Luke 22:39–46). Jesus, too, asked to be released from the passage into death; in the Epistle to the Hebrews we read that through his suffering, he becomes the source of eternal redemption (4:15). Saint Paul also speaks vividly of his own sufferings for the sake of the Gospel (2 Cor 11:24–28); he writes, "I will rather boast of my weaknesses, in order that the power of Christ may dwell in me" (2 Cor 12:9b). The prayer of Hezekiah, united with other texts of Scripture, helps us reflect on the meaning of suffering and its redemptive power in our lives—a passage in life that all of us must face.

Isaiah 38:10–14a, 17–20

10 I said: In the midst of my days I must depart.
I am consigned to the gates of Sheol
for the rest of my years.

11 I said, I shall not see
the LORD in the land of the living;
no more shall I look on the human race,
on those who inhabit the world.

12 My dwelling is pulled up and removed from me
like a shepherd's tent;
he has rolled up my life like a weaver,
who severs me from the last thread.
From dawn to dusk you bring me to an end.

13 I cry for help until morning.
Like a lion he crushes all my bones.
From dawn to dusk you bring me to an end.

14 Like a young swallow I murmur;
like a dove I moan.
My eyes grow weary gazing heavenward.

17 You saved my soul from the pit of destruction,
for you have cast behind your back all my sins.

18 For Sheol cannot give you thanks
nor can death give you praise;
nor can those who descend into the pit
hope any longer in your faithfulness.

19 The living, the living give you thanks
as I do this day.
Parents make known to their children your faithfulness.

20 The LORD is here to save me,
and we will sing to the sound of instruments,
all the days of our lives
in the house of the LORD.

Canticle Prayer

God, Creator and Bestower of Life, lead us in life's journey through the passages of suffering and death, that we may arrive at the full vision of your goodness and compassion. Through Christ our Lord

WEDNESDAY

1 Samuel 2:1–10

There Is No One as Holy as the Lord

In both the Old and New Testaments, the sacred authors distinguish men and women of faith by attributing prayers and canticles to them. We think of the canticles of Moses, Judith, Hezekiah, Daniel, the Virgin Mary, Zechariah, and Simeon, to name several of them. We turn our consideration now to the Canticle of Hannah, whose name and situation both bespeak a striking character of faith and perseverance. Her Hebrew name *Hannah* means "the favored one," but in the opening chapter of 1 Samuel she appears as anything but favored. As a barren or childless woman, Hannah is ridiculed and tormented by the second wife of her husband Elkanah; yet Elkanah loves her dearly in spite of her infertility; he shows her signs of special care and affection. At the temple of Shiloh, Hannah prays to God in fervent agitation, pleading for a male child and promising to establish him in the Lord's service. Seeing her fervent prayer, the priest Eli suspects that she is drunk on wine and admonishes her for making a spectacle. But when she explains the cause of her vigorous supplication, he offers her a word of hope: "Go in peace, and may the God of Israel grant your request" (1 Sam 1:17). The outcome of her situation is expressed almost tersely, yet it radiates divine tenderness and compassion: "...the LORD remembered her"

(1 Sam 1:19c). She who in the eyes of others was "not favored" has now been favored by the God to whom she has prayed so ardently.

In the Old Testament, people like Hannah are distinguished by poverty, lowliness, and simplicity united to a deep and persevering faith. They are called in Hebrew *anawim*, "the poor of the LORD." Such people demonstrate genuine righteousness, humility, fidelity, hope, meekness, steadfastness, and perseverance in the condition of their lives with trust in God's care for them. Both the Prophets and the Psalmists give special attention and recognition to these people. They attest in many ways to God's love of the poor (for examples, see Isa 3:15; 10:2; 11:4; 29:19; Pss 34:7, 19; 37:9, 11; 69:34; 72:4, 13; 82:4). Particularly in the Psalms, God acts as the protector and refuge of the poor and the needy; and it becomes the duty of the king, who acts as God's representative, to be sure that the poor receive the care that is the right of every human person.

The Canticle of Hannah demonstrates how one of God's "little ones" understands herself in relationship to the God who does all things for her and for all in need. She is able to rejoice, not in what she does, but in how God has saved her, given her new life, and raised her up from the dust. From beginning to end, this canticle exalts the One who has power over everyone and everything on the face of the earth. It is the LORD who bestows both wealth and prosperity, poverty and want. There is no place for the arrogant and haughty before God until they turn back to the Giver of all things and follow the divine word that comes through the Law and the Prophets. Within this vast and expansive universe, God carefully guides and cares for those who show themselves faithful and righteous at each step of their way (v. 9).

The evangelist Luke uses the motifs of Hannah's canticle to shape the story of the Blessed Virgin Mary, putting Hannah's words on her lips when she meets with her cousin Elizabeth

(Luke 1:46–55). The context is clear: Mary comes to the aid of her elderly relative in her unexpected pregnancy, a genuine act of loving kindness and compassion. This Canticle of Hannah invites all of us to praise and thank the God who touches our lives each day in ways subtle and stunning, humble and magnificent. What a blessing it is to acknowledge ourselves among the poor and needy who look to God for all our hopes and needs.

1 Samuel 2:1–10

1 My heart exults in the LORD;
my horn is exalted in my God.
My mouth derides my foes,
as I rejoice in your salvation.

2 There is no one as holy as the LORD;
truly, there is no one besides you,
and there is no rock like our God.
3 Speak no more with haughty pride,
nor let arrogance come forth from your mouth.
For the LORD is a God of knowledge,
and by him are actions weighed.

4 The bows of the mighty are broken,
while the feeble gird on strength.
5 The sated hire themselves out for bread,
while the hungry hunger no more.
The barren wife gives birth to seven,
while the one with many children is desolate.

6 The LORD deals death and brings to life,
casts down to Sheol and raises up.
7 The LORD makes poor and makes rich;
he brings down low yet lifts up high.

8 He raises the poor from the dust,
lifts the needy from the ash-heap,
to give them a seat with nobles,
to inherit a throne of glory.

For the pillars of the earth are the LORD's;
he has set the world upon them.
9 He guards the steps of his faithful ones,
but the wicked shall be silenced in darkness,
for not by strength is a warrior made mighty.

10 The LORD will shatter his foes,
against them will he thunder in the heavens.
The LORD will judge the ends of the earth,
will endow his king with strength,
and exalt the horn of his anointed.

Canticle Prayer

O God, our Savior and Redeemer, who lift up the lowly and heal the brokenhearted: grant us a knowledge of your gracious care for us, and keep us strong in our love and faithfulness to you, who live and reign forever and ever. Amen.

THURSDAY

Isaiah 12:1–6

The Holy One of Israel

This short but significant canticle of thanksgiving concludes that section of the Book of Isaiah that is often called the *Book of Emmanuel* (chaps. 9–12). These texts witness in hope to God's salvific action toward Judah and Jerusalem through the lineage of King David. The announcement in Isaiah 7:14 of the forthcoming Messianic figure whose name is Emmanuel (meaning in Hebrew "God is with us") prepares us for what follows in *The Book of Emmanuel*. Today we hear from these well-known passages during the Advent and Christmas seasons:

> The people who walked in darkness
> have seen a great light
>
> For a child is born to us, a son is given to us....
>
> A shoot shall sprout from the stump of Jesse,
> and from his roots a bud shall blossom.
> The spirit of the LORD shall rest upon him....
> He shall judge the poor with justice,
> and decide fairly for the land's afflicted....
> The calf and the young lion shall browse together,
> with a little child to guide them. (9:1, 5; 11:1–6 NABRE)

The canticle concludes with a restatement of the meaning of Emmanuel, God with us: "great in your midst is the Holy One of Israel." In the course of the liturgical year, Isaiah 12 serves eight times as a Responsorial Psalm at Mass and appears in the Liturgy of the Hours for special feasts of the Lord. This canticle celebrates the divine Presence that accompanies the people of God on their pilgrim journey through the challenges and blessings of life.

Reading slowly through this short canticle, one may discern in almost every line resonances of other Scripture texts: images and themes from throughout the Psalter, hymns from other books. As is typical of a canticle of thanksgiving, the prophet here explains that gratitude comes from God's anger turning back—quite literally, *divine conversion*—to ward off the devastating effects of war. The transformation of God's wrath into forgiveness becomes the true source of consolation and hope. In v. 2, the prophet acclaims God as "my salvation"—a personal expression of divine deliverance in his own life and in the lives of the people. In v. 3, "the springs of salvation" repeats the term *salvation*, urging us to reflect on its meaning and significance. The name "Isaiah" itself derives from a Hebrew root that means to save (*yaša'*); more emphatically, the LORD is salvation: indeed, the inspired seer affirms his belief in God's saving action toward Israel through every chapter of this prophetic book. *Salvation* is a common and familiar term in the books of the Old Testament, but what does it really mean in the original setting of the text? Salvation is a divine action by which a people, a nation, a city, a group, or even an individual experiences deliverance, victory, healing, liberation, forgiveness, or rescue from a life-threatening situation: looming death or annihilation, any potentially life-altering state of affairs. Salvation comes to pass through God's own choice and action. In the New Testament, Jesus Christ is acclaimed Savior of the human race through his saving passion, death, and resurrection. References to this profound sense of salvation are expressed in the writings of Paul, as well as by the evangelist Luke in his scene of the annunciation to the Virgin Mary (Luke 1:31–33, 35) and by Matthew in his scene of the annunciation to Joseph (Matt 1:21).

This section of the Book of Isaiah is set in the context of a threat against the national identity of Judah and Israel from Assyrian forces, which were subsequently subdued by divine intervention (Isa 37:36–37). Yet the story of Israel's experience of salvation continues to unfold in subsequent chapters of this prophetic book. Today, at this present moment, our own world continues to experience disruptive civil strife, devastating wars, deadly plagues, toxic environmental threats, continuing eruptions of centuries-old animosities, revelations of heinous crimes, and global anxiety about the future world left for coming generations. When we pray for a resolution to any of these overwhelming crises, we entreat God to bring salvation, to enter the human scene, and to lead our world in a direction that will bring peace, healing, and hope to all. Divine intervention seems an absolute necessity if we are to gain victory over any of these devastating problems. We can also see how the varied modes of divine deliverance, unforeseen and unexpected, enter into the individual lives of each of us. When we are struggling for years to find reconciliation with a friend or family member, we know that God alone can move hearts to bring saving grace to such painful situations. When we see injustice continuing to flourish, we know that divine wisdom alone can bring about the goodwill for people to come together and seek reasonable ways forward and create solutions agreeable to all. When we pray this canticle with the prophet, we sing praise to the One who alone works wonders, acknowledging that God is *my salvation*. In our midst is the Holy One of Israel (Isa 12:6).

Each morning in the Canticle of Zechariah, we attest that God has visited and redeemed us, the people of God, raising up for us a mighty Savior from the House of David, Jesus the Christ. And with Saint Paul, through the saving death and resurrection of Christ, we continue to experience the salvation that brings us forgiveness of our sins, an escape from eternal death, and the power of the Holy Spirit who abides within us, guiding us to live in accord with the Gospel. Indeed, salvation is an exalted term, yet it touches our lives each and every day and keeps us hoping for the divine intervention that will set us free to share in the glorious liberty of the children of God (Rom 8:21).

Isaiah 12:1–6

1 I give thanks to you, O Lord!
For though you were angry with me,
your anger turned back, and you consoled me.

2 Behold, God is my salvation!
I will trust and will not be afraid,

for the LORD is my strength and my praise,
and he has been my salvation.

3 With joy will you draw water
from the springs of salvation.

4 And you will say on that day:
Give thanks to the LORD, invoke his name;
make known among the peoples his deeds;
proclaim that his name is exalted.

5 Sing to the LORD for he has wrought wonders;
let this be known through all the earth.
6 Shout aloud and sing praise, you who dwell in Zion,
for great in your midst is the Holy One of Israel.

Canticle Prayer

God, mighty and merciful, continue to manifest your divine power in a world broken by sin, so that the mystery of your saving grace may be acknowledged and praised by all who experience your love and goodness. Through Christ our Lord and Savior. Amen.

FRIDAY

Habakkuk 3:2–4, 13a, 15–19

Yet Will I Rejoice

As a prayer, this canticle shows similarities to some of the psalms both in language and in theological motifs. The prophet begins his prayer by asking God to remember divine deeds of the past, along with their awe-inspiring consequences. To the

Hebrew mindset, calling on the LORD to remember earlier divine acts functions as a way both to praise and to petition God. The prophet speaks of God's past deeds as demonstrating a singular reputation of incomparable renown; no other deity has ever acted with such marvelous and unequaled power. Standing as a warrior for Israel, the Lord not only limits the strength of their enemies but manifests supreme power over nature itself. For these reasons, the prophet begs God to "renew" these magnificent deeds on their behalf. In other words, "Recall, O God, what you have done for us in the past and accomplish it again for us, now and in the future." A previous instance of approach employed here by the prophet is found in Psalm 44, where the people, having fallen into grave difficulties, remind God of the deeds once done on their behalf—foreign nations were driven out and victory brought about for Israel (Ps 44:2–9). Earlier in his prophecy, Habakkuk had described the injustice done by the Chaldeans against the people (2:9–17); now he asks God to recall the deeds of old; in the midst of this dire situation, he pleads for God's compassion.

In vv. 3–4, 13a, 15, the prophet describes the presence and activity of God as a *theophany*, a manifestation of the divine in their midst. When they observed the elements of nature deviating from familiar courses and rhythms, the ancients perceived this as a message being relayed to them by God. Theophanies demand the attention of those who experience them. In some cases a theophany serves as a warning; in others as a sign of divine presence or blessing. Perceiving and affirming God's presence among the people in their movement away from Teman and Mount Paran during their journey in the desert, the prophet uses language similar to that found in Deuteronomy 33:2, where the text describes the LORD coming from Mount Sinai to Paran, accompanying the Hebrew slaves to the promised land. The mention of God's "glory" suggests the immensity and substance of God's decisive act on behalf of the people. There is power in God's hand, and it is being manifested for the salvation of those in need.

Throughout the Scriptures, images of light signal the salvific act of God (see Pss 27, 36, 105; Isa 60). Here God's hand is described as holding within it a hidden power that is yet to be revealed. The prophet expresses the conviction that the imminent coming of God in mysterious and supernatural ways is for the salvation of the people; and yet, they must wait in distress and wonder for the full manifestation of God's presence (v. 16).

While the language of theophany at the heart of this prayer powerfully grips the reader, we see that both the opening and the closing of the prophetic words focus on a faith-filled and humble expression of trust in God's just and righteous action: we believe with the prophet that God will act in time. The prayer begins and concludes in the first-person voice of the prophet. "O LORD, I have heard of your fame; I am in awe, O LORD, of your work (v. 2)....Yet will I rejoice in the LORD, and rejoice in the God of my salvation" (v. 18). As the prophet manifests confidence in the justice of divine deliverance, he also demonstrates a faith that God will be with him even in moments of hardship. The prophet calls God "my strength," a profound recognition of divine action in his life; to show forth such trust and confidence is not the prophet's innate ability, but God's gift. When times are tough—when the trees fail to blossom, when the vine gives no yield, when crops fail, or flocks diminish to nothing—it is then that the prophet remembers what God has done in the past, and so trusts that such action will continue into the present and the future.

Throughout his ministry Saint Paul attests to that same belief: through hardship, God is present through the redeeming grace of Christ's resurrection (2 Cor 4:7–14). Whether by great theophanies or in the subtle promptings of the Holy Spirit, God speaks to us and calls us to faith in Jesus Christ, who is the Pioneer of our salvation. Living with such confidence, trust, and faith enables us to manifest God's strength at work in us, and to show forth our love for the God who continues to redeem us day after day.

Habakkuk 3:2–4, 13a, 15–19

2 O LORD, I have heard of your fame;
I am in awe, O LORD, of your work.
In the midst of the years, renew it.
In the midst of the years, make it known;
in your anger, remember compassion.

3 God is coming from Teman,
the Holy One from Mount Paran.
His glory covers the heavens;
and the earth is full of his praise.

4 His splendor is as the light:
rays come forth from his hand;
and there lies hidden his power.

13 You have come forth to save your people,
to save the one you have anointed....
15 You tread the sea with your steeds,
churning up the mighty waters.

16 I hear and quake to my inner depths;
my lips quiver at the sound.
Decay invades my bones;
and my steps beneath me tremble.
I await the day of distress,
for the people who come to attack us.

17 Though the fig tree fails to blossom,
or the vine to yield its fruit;
though the crop of the olive fails,
and the fields produce no grain;
though the flock is removed from the fold,
and there are no cattle in the stalls;

[18] yet will I rejoice in the LORD,
and rejoice in the God of my salvation.
[19] The LORD, my Lord, is my strength;
he makes my feet like those of the deer,
and makes me tread upon the heights.

Canticle Prayer

God of power and might, who reveal yourself in your mighty deeds and in the subtle movements of the Spirit within us: help us to know and experience Your strength as it guides us to abundant faith in your unending love for us. Through Christ our Lord.

SATURDAY

Deuteronomy 32:1–12

The name of the Book of Deuteronomy gives us a hint as to the aim and purpose of this canticle, one of several taken from that book. The word *Deuteronomy* comes from two Greek words: *deutero*, meaning second, and *nomos*, meaning law. As a kind of "second law," the Book of Deuteronomy gives us an insight into how God's law should be interpreted and why it should be lived. The biblical vision of Israel's covenant with God assured them of divine guidance and protection as long as they lived in accord with the expectations of the law. But the law was not to be understood as a mere set of precepts to be followed, a list of tasks without internal significance, a set of hoops to be jumped through. Rather the commandments were a gift to Israel: if they kept them, they were assured of divine deliverance and an identity in the LORD, a personal relationship with the one, true, and only God. The Book of Deuteronomy recounts numerous instances of how God's love and care for Israel gives them reason for following the law with faith and joy. It tells of Israel's history with constant reference to

God's loving care, abiding presence, and continuous protection. At times, it points out how God's goodness has been neglected, unappreciated, and ignored by the chosen people.

The canticle is attributed directly to Moses, who reminds the people of their relationship with the LORD. He begins in a solemn fashion, calling on the heavens and the earth themselves to listen attentively to his words, such that what he says will find a resting place within them (vv. 1–3). The tone is set in vv. 3–4: it immediately contrasts God's constant fidelity with Israel's betrayal of the LORD's justice and uprightness. The language is forceful on both matters, adulating God as great, loving, and caring, but berating Israel as a people corrupt, depraved, and perverse, once wise but fallen into foolishness in their relationship with the One who brought them into being. It is interesting to note here the variety of images used to portray God. First, God is a Rock, whose strength assures the people of something stable and enduring (v. 4). Second, God is depicted as a parent in both masculine and feminine terms. In v. 6b we read, "Is not he your Father who created you, who formed you and established you?" Then vv. 11–12 tell us, "As an eagle that brings out her nestlings, and hovers over her young, she spreads out her wings, takes them up, and bears them aloft on her pinions, so the LORD alone led him forth." Finally, we are reminded in the closing verse that it is the Lord alone who has done all these things for Israel: "there was no foreign god beside him" (v. 12b).

Two additional themes appear that can be a rich source for reflection: divine election and prophetic announcement. Divine election speaks of God's choice of the Hebrew people, enslaved by the Egyptians, and how he names them "his very own portion" (v. 9). On a human level, we can appreciate the experience of being selected to take on some position of honor or responsibility: this "election" distinguishes us, sets us apart from others in a special way. Among the nations of the Ancient Near East, many were stronger, larger, and more influential than Israel—a motley group of slaves who found themselves captive in Egypt through strange and unforeseeable circumstances. And yet, God chooses these people; the divine love in which God holds them is manifested in deliverance, in guidance through "a barren howling waste" (v. 10), and in the promise of a land to call their own. In prophetic language, this canticle not only speaks of what has happened to Israel and how God has saved them in the past but also hints at what is to come in their future. But despite the promise and fulfillment of God's faithful love for them, Israel will slip back into infidelity, ingratitude, and countless violations of the covenant agreement. Even though the Hebrew slaves passed safely through the desert of Sinai and entered into the promised land, their failure would be repeated in their history as God brings them through another desert—their slavery to the Babylonians—always showing faithful love and care for them (cf. Isa 40:1–5).

This Canticle of Moses rehearses for the people all that God has done for them, why they should be thankful, and why their obedience to the law should be a grateful response to God's gracious care for them. They had to *learn* how God manifests divine goodness; they must discover their proper response as a community chosen to show the world the vastness of God's mercy and compassion. And that remains an important lesson for us today. We need only look back and consider the history of our own lives, reflecting on how God's deliverance has entered into and erupted from our personal and communal experiences. In such reflection we find the reasons for gratitude, for renewal of heart, and for a hopeful future. Saint Paul writes of this experience when addressing the Ephesians: "That is not how you *learned* Christ" (4:20). Paul emphasizes that renewal of heart comes from a consideration of our former way of life: in discovering the justice, righteousness, and truth present in the life and example of Jesus Christ, we are brought to renewal of heart. That is how we *learn* God, how we follow God's ways, how we live Christ's example. The Canticle of Moses sets a tone that invites us to see the movement of God's grace that has animated both the lives of the chosen people and our own lives as well. As we come to discover ever more deeply the ways of God in our lives, we can be inspired to follow the One who leads us, guides us, and loves us as we, too, make our way through the deserts and oases that we encounter in our journey.

Deuteronomy 32:1–12

1 Give ear, O heavens, and I will speak;
O earth, hear the words of my mouth.
2 May my teaching soak in like the rain,
my discourse spread like the dew,
as gentle rain on fresh grass,
as showers on a field.

3 For the name of the LORD I will invoke;
acknowledge the greatness of our God!
4 The Rock, how perfect his deeds,
for all his ways are just;
a faithful God without deceit:
he is just and upright.

5 Yet his children have sinned and are corrupt,
a depraved and perverse generation.
6 Is this how you repay the LORD,
O people, foolish and unwise?
Is not he your Father who created you,
who formed you and established you?

7 Remember the days of old,
recall the years of past generations;
ask your father, and he will inform you,
your elders, and they will tell you:

8 when the Most High allotted the nations,
when he apportioned the children of Adam,
he established the boundaries of the peoples,
by the number of the children of Israel.
9 For the portion of the LORD is his people;
Jacob is the lot of his inheritance.

10 He found him in a region of the desert,
in a barren howling waste.
He enwrapped him and cared for him;
as the apple of his eye, he guarded him.

11 As an eagle that brings out her nestlings,
and hovers over her young,
she spreads out her wings, takes them up,
and bears them aloft on her pinions,
12 so the LORD alone led him forth,
and there was no foreign god beside him.

Canticle Prayer

God of wisdom and truth, who by the Spirit dwelling within us guide us in the ways of your providence: enable us to discern this loving presence in our lives, so that we may respond by following joyfully your new law of love in the circumstances of each day. Through Christ our Lord.

WEEK 3

SUNDAY

Daniel 3:57–88, 56

The Marvelous Works of the Lord

THIS CANTICLE IS prayed on both the First and Third Sundays of the four-week cycle of Morning Prayer. An initial consideration of this canticle appears in Sunday, Week 1, where the context of the canticle's scene and moment in history is noted. As this second treatment shows, consideration of its literary form provides an additional way to understand and pray the canticle as it appears on Sunday at Morning Prayer. The literary form of a biblical text often provides insight into how it has been used—and continues to be used—in liturgical celebrations. Many scholars of the Psalter regard Psalm 136 as a communal hymn of thanksgiving: in a recitation of the saving events of Israel's history, a refrain is inserted after each divine action is recalled—"for [God's] mercy [or love, or faithfulness, or kindness] endures forever." Thus the psalm takes the form of a litany—another literary form that helps us understand how this canticle may be prayed, and how its message is to be particularly appreciated on Sunday, the Lord's Day.

A litany is a series of petitions or expressions of praise, after each of which a response of gratitude or entreaty follows. These elements—petition or praise, followed by gratitude or entreaty—

may take several forms. The repetitive nature of the responses serves to emphasize the element they follow. For example, our contemporary Litany of the Saints presents a list of holy men and women, each of whom is implored for intercession—"pray for us"—regarding whatever the occasion calls for; at a profession of religious vows, an ordination to the priesthood, or an episcopal ordination, we beg the saints for prayers on behalf of the one being thus consecrated. After the list of saints is completed, specific petitions also relating to the occasion are met with a new form of response: "hear our prayer." This canticle calls on the whole of creation in all its variety of creatures to lift up praise and gratitude for the wonders worked by the mighty hand of God, who is worthy of all praise and exaltation.

Might we ourselves not adapt the literary form of the litany as we pray personally in the silence following the recitation of the canticle? For each of us, various ways in which we might pray from this litany may arise. We might ask God to make us thankful performers in the symphony of creation, joining our fellow creatures in the praise of God's goodness. We might recall occasions of gratitude when we have seen the hand of God at work in our own lives. We might think of how the power of God guides and shapes world events in the present day—in ways that cannot be accomplished by merely human efforts, ways that we may not even understand. We might ask divine assistance by placing before God blessings for which we ardently long, knowing that only God can fulfill our greatest hopes. A litany can open our hearts to attend to the many blessings that enter our lives each day. May our own litany be strong in faith, deep in hope, grateful in love, and enduring in its praise of God's goodness.

Daniel 3:57–88, 56

57 Bless the Lord, all you works of the Lord,
praise and highly exalt him forever.

58 Heavens, bless the Lord,
59 angels of the Lord, bless the Lord.
60 All waters above the heavens, bless the Lord,
61 all powers, bless the Lord.

62 Sun and moon, bless the Lord,
63 stars of heaven, bless the Lord.
64 Every shower and dew, bless the Lord,
65 all winds, bless the Lord.

66 Fire and heat, bless the Lord,
67 cold and heat, bless the Lord.
68 Dew and rain, bless the Lord,
69 frost and cold, bless the Lord.

70 Ice and snows, bless the Lord,
71 nights and days, bless the Lord.
72 Light and darkness, bless the Lord,
73 lightnings and clouds, bless the Lord.

74 Let the earth bless the Lord,
praise and highly exalt him forever.

75 Mountains and hills, bless the Lord,
76 all that grows on the earth, bless the Lord.
77 Seas and rivers, bless the Lord,
78 springs of water, bless the Lord.

79 Sea beasts and all that move in the water, bless the
Lord,
80 all birds of heaven, bless the Lord.
81 All wild beasts and cattle, bless the Lord,
82 all you people, bless the Lord.

83 O Israel, bless the Lord,
praise and highly exalt him forever.

84 Priests of the Lord, bless the Lord,
85 servants of the Lord, bless the Lord.
86 Spirits and souls of the just, bless the Lord,
87 holy and humble of heart, bless the Lord.
88 Hananiah, Azariah, Mishael, bless the Lord,
praise and highly exalt him forever.

Let us bless the Father, and the Son, with the Holy
Spirit.
Let us praise and highly exalt him forever.
56 Blessed are you in the firmament of heaven,
worthy of praise and highly exalted forever.

Canticle Prayer

Almighty God, Ruler of the universe, whose providential hand guides the course of history: hear our humble prayer for peace in the world. Though tempted to fear that our cries may be lost among the countless pleadings that rise before you, we know that you hear each one who calls on you in faith. We entrust to you our needs, confident that your loving care will never fail. May our words praise and thank you, now and forever. Amen.

MONDAY

Isaiah 2:2–5

Swords into Ploughshares

Despite its brevity, this canticle from the Book of Isaiah may be the most familiar of the prophet's numerous canticles. The famous text of Isaiah 2:4b, "They shall beat their swords into plowshares, and their spears into pruning hooks. Nation shall not lift up sword against nation, and they shall never again learn war," is engraved on a wall facing the United Nations building in New York. In the UN garden nearby, a sculpture depicts a man hammering the weapon of war into a farming tool; the statue was cast by Soviet artist Yevgeny Vuchetich in the midst of the Cold War era following the Second World War, emblematizing the prophetic call for peace. The words of this canticle (with slight variations) are also found in Micah 4:1–3. Micah's oracle emerges at around the same time as the opening chapters of Isaiah, with the rise of the Southern Kingdom of Judah and Assyrian threats against the Northern Kingdom of Israel (ca. 734–701 BCE).

This prophetic canticle comprises three important messages: (1) it is God's will that all nations enjoy the benefits of divine salvation; (2) the way to peace requires both the abolition of war and the establishment of God's teaching; and (3) Jerusalem is to be exalted as the place of God's dwelling. The opening verses emphasize that "all the nations" will come together as they "stream toward" Jerusalem. The same vision is portrayed in grand style in Isaiah 60, the high point of the whole of Isaian prophecy. Speaking of daughter Jerusalem, the prophet declares, "Nations shall walk by [Jerusalem's] light, kings by the radiance of your dawning....For the riches of the seas shall be poured out before you, the wealth of nations shall come to you" (Isa 60:3, 5b). Thus the movement of the nations toward Jerusalem, initiated at the outset of Isaiah's prophecy, will carry through the book even to the final chapter, giving voice to God's universal call to salvation: "I am coming to gather all nations and tongues, they shall come and see my glory....They shall bring all your kin from all the nations to Jerusalem, my holy mountain" (Isa 66:18, 20). In the closing verses of chapter 66 we read, "From new moon to new moon, and from sabbath to sabbath, All flesh shall come to worship before me, says the LORD" (v. 23). Isaiah's vision bespeaks God's purpose to unite the nations in that specific place where the divine presence most particularly dwells: the temple on Mount Zion in Jerusalem.

The canticle presents a forceful juxtaposition of the elimination of the instruments of war and instruction in the ways of God's plan for the future. The word translated here as *instruction* is the Hebrew word for *law* (*tôrâ*). Today's understanding of *law* usually suggests binding rules of conduct that bear some sense of authority and expectation. But the biblical sense of *law*, especially in relation to God's law, bears instead a sense of God's teaching the people how to act. The following of divine instruction provided Israel with direct knowledge of God; in following the law, the people of God came to know the very mind and heart of God—that is, what was expected of them by the Divine Author with whom they were covenanted. Keeping the law was Israel's way of living out its part of the covenant relationship first established by God; the people who followed the law were espoused to God. Likewise, Isaiah's prophecy shows that God's law is a gift to those who embrace it: they come to know in the law the ways of God, the ways to peace through the cessation of violence and war.

Throughout the Book of Isaiah, Jerusalem represents the place of God's dwelling; specifically, God's dwelling among the human race in the temple on Mount Zion. Those who have had an opportunity to visit Jerusalem have seen that, in contrast to what the text of Isaiah says, Mount Zion is not the highest mountain of the region. The Psalmist reminds us that Jerusalem is surrounded by more significant mountains, and thus protected by them (Ps 125:1–2). The prophet envisions a day when the nations will stream to the sacred city, having seen what God has done for Israel; they will want to share in God's protection in this covenant relationship, by learning and living the divine law. As the dwelling place of God, Jerusalem is where the peoples will want to find a new home, to share in the divine judgment that will end wars among the nations, bring peace that God intends for all human beings, and establish the nonviolent relations that are a hallmark of God's kingdom. As the canticle closes, God invites the house of Jacob to walk in light—a symbol of salvation. God's people will lead the way to salvation in living by God's loving instruction; on their example is founded the hope that other nations will learn to do the same, and so come to know the meaning of God's covenant, which promises deliverance, an end of war, protection, and security.

Could there ever be a time when this canticle does not stir us to pray and work for an end to war and violence, not only in Jerusalem but throughout the whole earth? Almost three thousand years old, this canticle remains a beacon over the troubled waters of civil strife, nationalism, conflicts among peoples, worldwide pandemics, and a future that remains uncertain in the search for world peace. The canticle reminds us that in the end God stands as the final judge in all such matters; and we can count on a judgment that is just and loving, righteous and wise, prudent, and compassionate for all God's children. Let us pray that we may always be God's instruments, helping to build peace each day in our own corner of the world.

Isaiah 2:2–5

2 It will happen in the latter days
that the mountain of the house of the LORD
will be established as the highest mountain
and will be raised above the hills.

Then all the nations shall stream toward it;
3 and many peoples shall come and say,
"Come, let us go up to the mountain of the LORD,
to the house of the God of Jacob,
that he may instruct us in his ways,
and we may walk in his paths."

For out of Zion shall go forth instruction,
and the word of the LORD from Jerusalem.

[4] And he will judge between nations,
and decide terms for many peoples.

And they shall beat their swords into plowshares,
and their spears into pruning hooks.
Nation shall not lift up sword against nation,
and they shall never again learn war.

[5] O house of Jacob, come,
let us walk in the light of the LORD.

Canticle Prayer

God of all nations, Creator of all peoples, look lovingly upon all who seek to walk in your ways, and bestow upon them your guidance and blessing. Keep us attentive to your instruction, that we may be moved by your light through the darkness of doubt and uncertainty, finally obtaining the vision of your will for the whole human race. Through Christ our Lord.

TUESDAY

Isaiah 26:1b–4, 7–9, 12

Waiting and Yearning

Canticles from the Book of Isaiah continue for several days at Morning Prayer during this third week in the Liturgy of the Hours. This canticle opens with reference to "a city strong in salvation," which for most readers immediately suggests Jerusalem. While the city mentioned here probably does refer to that city, it is worth noting that Jerusalem is not explicitly named anywhere in this chapter of Isaiah. That fact in itself suggests that we might want to consider reading this canticle from a fresh perspective.

In its scriptural context, the canticle includes an introductory phrase that is omitted for recitation in prayer; these initial words, however, provide an important clue to understanding the canticle. The phrase reads, "On that day this song will be sung in the land of Judah" (Isa 26:1a). Throughout the prophetic literature, "on that day" is a stock expression that designates some significant future event, an act of divine scope and magnitude. It indicates an eschatological pronouncement. God will turn the tide of history with power and might, manifesting deliverance in an unexpected intervention that alters the course of salvation history. And while the unnamed city may be Jerusalem, the passage is constructed more generally: our attention is focused on the forceful hand of God acting at a significant moment in Israel's story. Thus we can infer that the canticle speaks of divine intervention in the life of God's people throughout Judah without restricting its message to Judah's most significant city.

First and foremost, the God of Israel is a God of salvation. The speakers affirm that their city is strong on account of God's action on their behalf. In the description of the physical features of the city, the walls and ramparts signify divine victory. It is not by human strength that this city establishes itself in peace but by the loving and merciful promise of God to deliver the people in fulfillment of the covenant promise. The closing line of the canticle expresses clear belief that God has faithfully accomplished all that has come about to make it strong: "O Lord, you order peace for us; for you accomplished all our works for us" (Isa 26:12). The reference to peace—*shalom* in Hebrew—bears a sense beyond the mere absence of anxiety: in its biblical context, *shalom* implies well-being, a right ordering of life, a sense of harmonious living, an equilibrium that promises concord, a security against enemies. The gift of *shalom* conveys the wonders of salvific grace bestowed by God in loving care.

The theme of righteousness emerges in several expressions in the canticle. "Open the gates so that a nation that is righteous…

may enter" (v. 2); "the path of the righteous is level; you make smooth the course of the righteous one" (v. 7); "the world's inhabitants learn righteousness" (v. 9c). Today, the word *righteous* often bears a negative connotation for some because they associate it with *self-righteousness*. Yet righteousness holds a place of manifest importance in biblical usage: it means a morally just, honest, upright, and blameless standard of life. Righteousness is frequently employed to describe divine action; examples may be found in Psalms 7:18, 111:3, and 116:5 as well as Tobit 3:2. The righteousness of God gives direction to those who would call themselves God's people; as God is righteous, so the people of God must follow the path of righteousness in daily living.

The prophet expresses a desire to experience closeness to God. "My soul yearns for you in the night; my spirit within me seeks you at dawn" (v. 9). Having experienced God's saving presence, desire for even more intimacy with the Lord naturally follows. The prophet calls for trust in God's ways (v. 4): in the mysterious movements of life, there is only one way in which to experience the grace, mercy, and goodness of God, whose loving care is as solid as a rock (v. 4). Affirmations of God's loving care for the people provide the reasons on which they readily base their trust. It is as if the prophet says, "Consider all that the Lord has done for us; our response must be trust, to trust God forever."

We began our consideration of this canticle by discerning in it a testimony of God's divine action in the lives of the people of Judah. Though they have strayed from God's ways, the All Holy One has remained faithful, manifesting divine righteousness by bringing them victory over their enemies and establishing peace on their borders. As we recite this canticle, the words of the prophet invite us to look at the ways in which God has touched our world, our nations, our families, and our very lives—especially in this difficult moment in global history. This moment can become a time for us to see in particular and distinct ways how God's saving action has been communicated in the world around us and within us. Can we ever fully enumerate those ways? We can never fully number the endless manifestations of divine love we have experienced; we can only burst forth in a litany of gratitude and praise.

Isaiah 26:1b–4, 7–9, 12

1 Ours is a city strong in salvation;
he has set up walls and bulwarks.
2 Open the gates so that a nation that is righteous,
one that keeps faith, may enter.

3 You guard the steadfast mind in peace,
in peace, for its trust is in you.
4 Trust in the Lord forever and ever;
an everlasting Rock is the LORD.

7 The path of the righteous is level;
you make smooth the course of the righteous one.
8 Yes, in the path of your judgments,
we wait for you, O LORD;
your name and your renown
are the desire of the soul.

9 My soul yearns for you in the night;
my spirit within me seeks you at dawn.
When your judgments are wrought on earth,
the world's inhabitants learn righteousness.

12 O LORD, you order peace for us;
for you accomplished all our works for us.

Canticle Prayer

Lord God, whose ways are peace and righteousness, help us amid the many changes of this world to see ever more clearly the working of your mighty and loving hand. Strengthen our faith to discern your presence in our world and in our lives, that we may petition you aright in gratitude for your endless goodness toward us. Through Christ our Lord.

WEDNESDAY

Isaiah 33:13–16

Bread and Water Assured

By employing terms like *fear, trembling, the godless, devouring fire*, and *everlasting flames*, this canticle quickly establishes an ominous mood of dread and doom suitable for a scene of judgment. The prophetic writings typically manifest a constant concern that the people truly live out the expectations of the covenant, adhering to the law codes and their interpretations. The prophets knew God's voice in the giving of the law, and they were compelled to point out to the people their failures to uphold and observe the divine precepts. What kept these prophetic words alive through so many generations? Throughout its history, at those all-too-frequent times when the people strayed from God's instruction, Israel was compelled to recognize the fulfillment of the prophets' words in the devastating events that subsequently befell them. Thus they came to see the truth in God's call that came to them through the prophets, believing that these words would be important for future generations to follow with faith and trust.

In this canticle from Isaiah, the prophet speaks in a language that foresees divine intervention, a moment of judgment—even as an eschatological warning for the end-times. God speaks, telling the people to acknowledge the divine and mighty hand they see at work, even if from far away. Those who have been at a distance from God's instructions are now caught; their experience is fear and dread—a physical trembling before the deeds of God. Implicit in the image is an early understanding of the place of punishment for evil and wicked deeds: a consuming fire of eternal flames—other examples can be found Isaiah 5:24; 9.17–18; 10:16–17. But then the text immediately proceeds with words of instruction from the prophet, calling them to walk in God's ways. The image of walking represents the hearer's manner of life, as in Psalm 1. In other words, to "walk rightly" means to act righteously in keeping with the covenant and all that it entails.

The prophet's words distinguish ways of acting: with righteous deeds, speaking—in truth and honesty; and choosing—what is right, honorable, and moral. These aspects of moral conduct initially show a positive approach to one's way of life. But the prophet clearly adds that to follow the ways of God also means avoiding what is wrong, evil, or unjust: taking a bribe, ignoring evil when it does occur, or closing one's eyes when wrong deeds call for a just response. The prophet brings all of these ideas together in a single verse. Here Isaiah suggests that silence in the face of injustice makes us accomplices when we could have made a difference for the good. Here the prophet has become something akin to the conscience of the people, calling forth from them a way of conduct that clearly aligns them with the vision of God's own uprightness and benevolence. In the passing of each day, so many occasions arise when we can act for the good of others, building up a world of peace, harmony, and goodwill.

Isaiah 33:13–16

13 Hear what I have done, O you who are far off;
and you who are near, acknowledge my might.

14 Sinners in Zion are shaking with fear;
trembling seizes the godless.
"Who of us can dwell with the devouring fire;
who of us can dwell with everlasting flames?"

15 The one who walks rightly and speaks honestly,
who spurns what is gained by oppression,
who shakes his hand free lest it accept a bribe,
who closes his ears not to listen to bloodshed,
who shuts his eyes not to gaze on evil.

16 Such a one shall dwell upon the heights,
whose refuge will be a rocky stronghold,
whose bread will be given, and whose water assured.

Canticle Prayer

Divine Spirit, dwelling within us: guide us in the ways of goodness, truth, and mercy; enable us to speak the truth in love; lead us to walk the paths of justice; let us see with eyes that penetrate the deepest meanings of what is before us; make us true servants in imitation of Jesus Christ, who lives and reigns forever and ever. Amen.

THURSDAY

Isaiah 40:10–17

Like a Shepherd

This canticle is recorded in the second section of the Book of Isaiah (chaps. 40–55), the text often called the Book of Consolation. The prophet's proclamations present striking images of a people captive in Babylon, awaiting a word of hope. Isaiah 40 opens with the words, "Comfort, give comfort to *my people*, says *your God*." From this passage hope springs forth. The people had broken their covenant with God, but God now subtly repeats the divine offer: you will be *my people*, and I will be *your God*. In regard to the road back to Jerusalem, the text foretells an act of divine power—valleys made level and mountains reduced to plains (Isa 40:4). All flesh shall behold God's word fulfilled.

It is in this context of good news—news of something done by God breaking forth—that our canticle begins, here in the midst of the chapter. In vv. 10–11, the song sets forth the image of God's assistance coming forth as a combination of divine power and pastoral care. The image of God's arm (v. 10) signifies divine power and control. And yet the hand of God wielding mighty power is also the hand of a shepherd who feeds, gathers together, and leads his flock with an intimacy bespeaking God's affectionate tenderness. Initially we might well understand this image as presenting tenderness for a people at a critical moment—as exile surely suggests. And yet if we examine as a whole the movement of the biblical texts—both Old and New Testaments—we see that God constantly shepherds the people through desert and darkness, bringing them to a land of promise. This theme thus runs the length and breadth of Scripture. Here, God once again shepherds the people of the covenant back to the promised land. In the New Testament, Jesus presents himself as the model shepherd, whose care and concern for the flock distinguishes God's own attitude toward the people, redeemed again and again.

The canticle rhetorically separates vv. 10–11 from vv. 12–27: the theme of divine power and might is sustained, but its expression is given a distinct literary form. In vv. 12–14, a series of rhetorical questions suggests to us the many ways in which God's creative power has been at work since the beginning of creation. Again, the image of a divine hand serves to show how God's power first brought into action the divine plan for the whole of creation—and how it continues to do so. In this way Isaiah manifests for us a sense of the divine will for the well-being of all creation and for God's people in particular. From whom must God ask knowledge or insight that these things might be accomplished? Has the God of Israel sought counsel from any among the deities of the ancient world? Whom did God need to consult regarding decisions about the elements of creation in their movements through space and time? Clearly, the answer is—no one! Thus trust, fidelity, and confidence belong alone to the God of Israel; and thus there is every reason for each and every creature, for each and every nation—including the people of God—now and always to trust in the divine plan.

The canticle concludes with a further description of the world as God created it, and how that world relates to the life of Israel. When we consider how God, again and again, has saved and redeemed Israel, we see that all the nations of the world are as nothing more than a drop in a bucket (v. 15). The prophet goes on to consider Lebanon's forests, especially its famous cedars—recognized as having extraordinary status in the world known to Israel. These were especially valued for their many and multiple uses—as wood for fuel, as timber for implements of agriculture or war, as building material for many structures of significant magnitude. But valuable as they are, they count as nothing before the God of all creation—who is also singularly the God of Israel. The passage thus bears a special and important message for our own time. As we see so many different institutions of power in our world today—nations, peoples, churches, cultures, economies—facing times of strife, hardship, violence, and uncertainty, we recognize the call to an ever-deeper faith in God who alone can guide the world and all that is in it. At the same time, God has endowed each of us with spiritual and humane wisdom that leads us to see how each of us can make a difference in our own small corner of the world. God is in charge, but we are God's instruments.

Isaiah 40:10–17

10 Behold, the Lord GOD comes with might,
and his arm is ruling for him;
behold, his reward is with him,
and his recompense before him.

11 Like a shepherd he feeds his flock;
he gathers the lambs in his arms,
and in his bosom he carries them;
he gently leads the ewes.

12 Who can measure out the waters with his hand,
and mark out the heavens with a span,
and gauge the earth's dust with a measure,
and weigh the mountains with scales,
and the hills with a balance?

13 Who has directed the Spirit of the LORD,
or who has taught him as his counselor?
14 Whom did he consult to gain understanding,
and who taught him in the path of judgment,
and who could teach him knowledge,
and make known to him the way of understanding?

15 Behold, the nations are but a drop from a bucket,
and are reckoned as dust on the scales;
behold, he lifts up the islands like fine powder.
16 There is not enough in Lebanon to burn,
nor its beasts enough for whole burnt offerings.

17 All the nations are as nothing to him;
as emptiness and nothing he accounts them.

Canticle Prayer

O God, Shepherd and almighty Lord, who manifest your loving kindness both in tenderness and in power, enable us to see with eyes of faith to discern your workings in our world today. As we experience your boundless grace and goodness, strengthen us to proclaim your divine justice and all-holy righteousness in the ways by which we fashion our own lives and contribute to the lives of those around us. Through Christ our Lord.

FRIDAY

Jeremiah 14:17–21

Hope for Healing

This short passage from the Book of Jeremiah is in fact a dialogue; to understand the text properly, special attention must be paid to identifying the speakers. The first of the two speakers appears in vv. 17–18, and the second in vv. 19–21. The words used by the speaker in vv. 17–18 betray powerful emotions cast in recognizably biblical language; this construction distinguishes a tragic moment in Israel's history. The opening words of the canticle comprise a *lament*—a biblical genre that expresses a speaker's deep sorrow as it arises from a judgment that has come upon the people. Yet the format of the text presents a question for the reader: Who is speaking here? Is it the prophet? Is it God? Or is it the prophet speaking in God's name? Scholars differ in their interpretation of who actually speaks these emotionally charged verses. My own sense is that in this passage it is God who is speaking through the prophet. God weeps, day and night, over the people who, brought into being by divine power and will, nonetheless fall away from their origin and source. The grievous wound that they bear is the distance their sin has brought about between God and themselves.

The last two lines of v. 18 put forth the cause of this disaster. When the text says that both priest and prophet walk the land without knowledge, it is clear that something serious has happened. First of all, the invoking of priest and prophet calls to mind those who are leaders of the people from a spiritual perspective. The word *knowledge* must be read in the context of the prophetic writings. For the prophet, *knowledge* is understanding of God, comprehension of the Lord's ways, and relationship with the All Holy One. In the Scriptures, especially in the Prophets and the Psalms, knowledge is far more than mere facts or information; knowledge constitutes a singular level of relationship, especially with regard to God. In the Bible, knowing a person involves a great degree of intimacy—especially when that person is God. For example, when Jeremiah comes to understand that the Lord *knew* him before he was formed in the womb (Jer 1:5), that understanding implies an intimate relationship between himself and God, who will call him to rise and take on the role of prophet, one who speaks for God. So here in Jeremiah 14:15, the implication is that the priest, the prophet, and the people of the land have lost their way with respect to their relationship with God. The covenant calls for fidelity to God's law, a fidelity that manifests their loyalty and relationship to God not just as lawgiver but as *person*. In failing to follow the precepts of the covenant, the people have brought this upon themselves, for in their breaking of the covenant they have excluded themselves from the favor of God. The disease, famine, and death they encounter become their own self-imposed judgment for having forsaken God's law.

The lament continues in vv. 19–21, but it is now on the lips of the people of Judah. The text moves through a series of questions that the people pose to God. They express the pain and suffering they feel in their distance from God, who once was their protector in the covenant relationship they shared with the Lord. The language is strong, expressing clearly a sense of rejection, of knowing that the only way out of their dire situation will be through divine healing. But will it come? In their moment of abject terror, all they feel is the absence of God's care for them, and the question cannot be answered positively. But then in v. 20, the people acknowledge not only their own wicked deeds but also those of their ancestors. Closing the verse, the people confess that they have sinned against God. The Hebrew verb *chata'* here expresses the people's acknowledgment that they have, literally, missed the mark, failed in their observance, and broken their relationship with God.

The final verse (v. 21) begs God to turn back and show divine compassion. The expression, "for the sake of your name," implies that their plea includes the request that God manifest all that the divine name implies and shows forth: mercy, compassion, divine justice, loving kindness, faithfulness, and slowness to anger (cf. Exod 34:6–7). Though it appears that the people have failed in their observance of the covenant, they nonetheless call upon God to remember the covenant once made between the Lord and their ancestors, and not to break those bonds that set them apart as a people.

As we indicated at the beginning of this reflection, there are two laments expressed here: God's own lament, and the people's lament. It can be a worthwhile spiritual exercise to consider God's own self-expression to the prophet of utter sadness. The idea of divine tears is a powerful image, giving us much to reflect upon. What can possibly cause divine tears? Can we imagine that such tears might also flow from the eyes of God today? In a world of broken promises, of failures to heed the Gospel's invitation to new life, there is certainly much to ponder.

Jeremiah 14:17–21

[17] Let my eyes overflow with tears,
night and day, may they not cease,
for the virgin daughter of my people

is afflicted with a great affliction,
a most grievous wound.

18 If I go out to the field,
behold, those slain by the sword.
And if I enter the city,
behold, diseases from famine.
Both the prophet and the priest
have traversed the land without knowledge.

19 Have you rejected Judah completely?
Does your soul detest Zion?
Why have you struck us down,
with no hope of our healing?
We wait for peace, but find no good;
for a time of healing, but see, terror.

20 We acknowledge our wickedness, O LORD,
the iniquity of our ancestors,
for we have sinned against you.

21 Do not spurn us, for the sake of your name,
nor dishonor your glorious throne.
Remember! Break not your covenant with us.

Canticle Prayer

O God, truly loyal and ever faithful, look upon the people of your covenant with compassion, mercy, and loving-kindness. We know and acknowledge our sins and failures, and likewise we confess your healing grace and peace. May we experience your love beyond our expectations, and never fail to be messengers to others of your forgiving love and mercy in our own lives. Through Christ our Lord.

SATURDAY

Wisdom 9:1–6, 9–11

Though One Be Perfect

The context of this canticle includes the events of 1 Kings 3, where we find an account of the beginning of Solomon's reign. Upon Solomon's blessing as king, God appears to him in a dream, inviting him to request anything at all, with the assurance of divine generosity and abundance (1 Kgs 3:5). Solomon asks for a *listening heart* (1 Kgs 3:9), so that he might exercise his service as one characterized by right judgment and just action. In the early chapters of the Book of Wisdom (see Wis 1:1–5), it is precisely this sound judgment and righteous deeds that are needed to face the challenges of the time and place in which the text was composed (usually thought to have been Alexandria in the first century BCE). The author describes how failure to observe these straightforward commands of God leads to death; wisdom is the necessary trait that will bring wholeness, discipline, virtue, and long life to the people of God. Just judgment and the search for integrity—these are the marks of wisdom established at the outset of the wisdom books.

It is interesting to note that the name of Solomon does not even appear in the text of this canticle; there is no clear statement that distinguishes the passage as his words, his prayer. The author did not deem it necessary to make explicit a fact that he supposed all of his readers to know: the identity of the one who was the inspiration behind the words. Likewise, the rhetorical structure of the book places the prayer in the middle of the Book of Wisdom, of which three distinct parts are evident: first, the need for just and righteous behavior in a situation threatened by increasing wickedness and inevitable death (Wis 1:1—6:21); second, admiration of and prayer for wisdom (6:22—10:21); and third, a *midrash* (a formal Jewish mode of interpretation applied to texts recounting historical experience) that tells the story of wisdom's role in the great exodus event (Wis 11:1—19:22). The prayer's placement in the middle of the book makes it the focal point—figuratively, the heart or centerpiece of the text.

As the heart of the ninth chapter of Wisdom, the canticle is a stirring and inspiring expression of Solomon's deep reflection on the experience of personified Wisdom and her specific activity. It is both poetry and profound prayer. It names the God who has abided with Israel's ancestors; the God who has created all things and given divine gifts to human beings. Wisdom receives from God the monumental task of governing the world in holiness, demonstrating always what is righteous. To "govern in holiness" is a biblical concept that requires some explanation. By its definition, holiness (Hebrew *qadosh*; Greek *hagios*) in its earliest biblical context refers to something that is set apart, uniquely Other, distinguishing what is sacred from what is profane. Thus "to govern the world in holiness" is to rule and preside as God would, exercising divine qualities of compassion, uprightness, righteousness, and justice. The image of a "consort of [God's] throne" (v. 4) suggests a harmonious working together between God and Wisdom in the process of ruling and making judgments. The Hebrew word for wisdom, *chokmah*, is feminine, as is its Greek equivalent, *sophia*. Thus the personified form is often addressed or referred to as Lady Wisdom, and the feminine pronouns *she* or *her* (see Prov 9:1–18; 31:10–31; Sir 1:1–10; 14:20–27; 24:1–33) are often employed in speaking of personified wisdom.

The prayer of Solomon asks for the wisdom to carry out what God intends for him to do; Solomon presents himself as God's servant—though a servant who is weak, and who lacks the experience of passing judgments that manifest true understanding of a given situation. And from this acute self-knowledge, he knows further that without wisdom, it would not be possible for him to carry out the tasks that must be his as king. Importantly, the text makes evident the depth of Solomon's prayer: he knows that he cannot by himself find or seek out wisdom; wisdom must be given by God, obtained from the Divine Source itself, for Wisdom is sent forth from the source of wisdom, the Divine One who created her and brought her into being.

The closing line bears in itself the profound implications of Solomon's situation as king. Solomon expresses his belief that Wisdom personified has *knowledge*—a personal experience regarding all things and the order in which they are meant by God to unfold. She guides with prudence both the actions to be taken by Solomon and the decisions he must make for the sake of others. The text of the canticle ends thus: "[she] will keep guard over me with her *glory*" (9:11c). We often think of *glory* as something bright, illuminating, and divine. These expressions are included in the biblical notion of *glory*, but the meaning here is perhaps more nuanced. As *doxa* (in Greek), or *kabod* (in Hebrew), "glory" implies literally a heavy weight, or more figuratively a solemn or serious matter. We might translate the phrase more loosely, or *periphrastically*, as, "[Wisdom] will keep guard over me in life's most challenging encounters." The use of "glory" here provides a powerful indication of the significance and impact of wisdom in the weightier decisions of life.

In the biblical mind, Wisdom is understood both as a person—specifically a woman—and as an interior disposition of the heart that enables one to see deeply into the questions and challenges of life, to evaluate life's experiences in light of God's law, and to treasure Wisdom as a companion in one's life journey. As one of God's gifts, Wisdom's worth is beyond compare (Prov 31:10–31).

Wisdom 9:1–6, 9–11

[1] O God of my ancestors, Lord of mercy,
who by your word have made all things,
[2] and in your wisdom have established man
to be master of the creatures you have made,

3 to govern the world in holiness and righteousness,
and to pass judgment with an upright heart,
4 grant me wisdom, the consort of your throne,
and reject me not from your children.

5 For I am your servant, the son of your handmaid,
a man who is weak and short-lived,
young in understanding of judgment and law;
6 though one be perfect among the children of Adam,
yet if wisdom from you be not with him,
he shall be regarded as nothing.

9 With you is wisdom who knows your works,
who was present when you made the world,
and comprehends what is pleasing in your eyes,
and what is right in accord with your commands.

10 O send her forth from the holy heavens;
from the throne of your glory dispatch her,
that she may be with me and labor at my side,
and I may know what is pleasing to you.

11 For she knows and understands all things,
and she will prudently guide me in my actions,
and will keep guard over me with her glory.

Canticle Prayer

God of Wisdom, God of Truth, who endow all your creatures with the light of your goodness, show us the way to understanding and a knowledge of You, that we may imitate your ways of holiness, and act under your guidance in life's challenges, thus helping to construct a world imbued with your mercy and peace. Through Christ our Lord.

WEEK 4

SUNDAY

Daniel 3:52–57

Praised and Exalted Forever

THE BIBLICAL AUTHOR'S admiration for God's creation, as well as the words of praise and thanksgiving it gives rise to in this canticle, have been with us for over two millennia. The ancients looked upon everything around them as marvels, thus developing their keen insight into the greatness of the God of Israel. For us in the twenty-first century, modern science has accumulated vast knowledge of the world in which we live. Increasing understanding of time and space, of the intricate processes of plant and animal life on land and in the sea, of changes in climate and environment, of the human body and even the mind itself, and knowledge of the new and constantly developing technologies through which we come to such understandings—this achievement, stunning and wondrous though it may be, nonetheless brings human beings to an abrupt standstill as we contemplate the Creator of this vast yet intelligible universe. Our faith reminds us that all we have and are comes to us as a gift from God (Jas 1:17). Everything in our world has its origin, development, and fulfillment in God. Thus these brief lines of praise in the Canticle of Daniel are appropriately given to us for our reflection on Sunday—the first of days, the beginning of creation—and the day of the new creation that comes to us in the resurrection of Jesus Christ.

A real and significant challenge can be discerned in these words of praise. Our lives are filled with gifts that we often take for granted, but with this canticle the Church invites us to penetrate more deeply the mystery of God's creation and its daily unfolding around us. In some ways, the wonders of creation are simply too much for us to hold continually before our eyes. Words will never fully capture the holiness that surrounds us in our lives, whether we encounter it in a visit to a museum of art or natural history, or on a leisurely walk through a park. Yet what an important practice it is for us to consider attentively the things we too often take for granted. As we gaze more carefully into the God-given mystery of things, as we open our hearts in praise of what we find all around us, we are ourselves drawn more deeply into the mystery in which we abide. When we can stand in awe of the simplest of things, and in them encounter the One who is their source, we come to discern in our own hearts the movement of profound praise for the Giver of these good gifts. The riches of life that encompass us call forth a response. And what is our response? Is it silence in awe before the plain and unpretentious things that are given by God for our well-being? Can we recognize that in our unmindfulness toward these many wonders, we can lose touch with the Creator of these good things?

On any given day we are obliged to face any number of challenges; the demands that such challenges place on us cannot be doubted. Yet many passages of Scripture, like these from the Book of Daniel, remind us that we owe our primary consideration to the glory of God. Each person and every thing has its origin in God; each has its own particular place in the divine plan for the world and all who dwell in it. As we read through the Psalms, encountering and indeed participating in the Psalmist's own trials and struggles, we are aware that each plea is directed to the One who can effect change in our situation. When the Psalmist cries out for help in circumstances far beyond his own strength or capability, his cries are always addressed to the One and only God who brings resolution—the God who governs both universally and in all particular circumstances.

A personal reflection that flows from this realization is that each Sunday—the day of resurrection and the affirmation of faith—is a unique day of praise for each Christian. This canticle is brief, its refrain even repetitive. Yet even so it lifts us from the world in which we find ourselves—a world full of suffering and pain, illness and loss, anguish and heartache, and endless uncertainty. It lifts us up and places us before God who knows all things, who brought us into being, who sustains us in our passages through life. It is all too simple to say, "We must praise and thank God for all that is, for all that has been, and for all that is to come." We have to look deep within our lives to recognize and acknowledge the experiences of new life and resurrection that enter into our experience to transform us. This canticle pushes aside the things that might undermine our wholehearted praise and thanks to God, an urge that comes from deep with the human person, from the heart. If every day, by simply looking around us, we can see why praise and thanks are due to God, how much more will this truth resound on Sunday—when we recall the gift of forgiveness and reconciliation that is ours through the cross and resurrection of Christ.

Daniel 3:52–57

52 Blessed are you, O Lord, the God of our ancestors,
to be praised and highly exalted forever.

Blessed is your glorious and holy name,
to be highly praised and exalted forever.

53 Blessed are you in the temple of your holy glory,
to be highly praised and glorified forever.

54 Blessed are you on the throne of your kingdom,
to be praised and highly exalted forever.

55 Blessed are you who look into the depths,
seated upon the cherubim,
to be praised and highly exalted forever.

56 Blessed are you in the firmament of heaven,
worthy of praise and highly exalted forever.

57 Bless the Lord, all you works of the Lord,
praise and highly exalt him forever.

Canticle Prayer

O God, our Creator and Redeemer, who from the beginning of time ordered all things for the wellbeing and care of your children: Strengthen our ability to discern in creation your loving and gracious care as it moves through our daily lives for our salvation. Through Christ our Lord.

MONDAY

Isaiah 42:10–16

The Lord Leads the Blind

This canticle echoes a phrase we hear several times in the Psalms and elsewhere in the prophetic writings, "Sing to the LORD a new song." This phrase conveys the message that God has touched the course of human history to bring redemption and deliverance to the people of Israel. Looking back at the opening of Isaiah 42, we recall that God has introduced an important person into the scene: the messianic figure known as God's Servant.

That expression, "Behold my Servant" inaugurates a series of four Servant Songs, each displaying a different presentation of this individual (or people), that runs through chapters 40–55 of Isaiah (cf. Isa 42:1–4; 49:1–6; 50:4–9a; 52:13—53:12). The Servant is identified as the mediator of justice (Isa 42:1–4), the prophet of salvation (Isa 49:1–6), the true disciple (Isa 50:4–9a), and the suffering and redeeming servant (52:13—53:12). In all these contexts, the Servant is one who carries out the Lord's own mission. The canticle of Isaiah 42:10–16 is a cry of exultation for what God is accomplishing in their midst: God's deliverance of the people of Judah, a kind of second exodus. It is a *new song*, a new hymn telling of the mysterious reality of God's glory and greatness. How worthy of praise is God in this new act: the liberation of the people from Babylonian powers.

The prophet uses evocative images to underscore the enormity and significance of God's deeds. Praise of God's act of deliverance will go out to the ends of the earth, to the depths of the sea, even to the little islands that dot its distant surfaces. The prophet goes to great lengths to assure his readers that this praise will reach every corner of the world. From the uninhabited desert to the populated cities, it resounds even in the villages of Kedar—a rocky and mountainous desert distinguished by notoriously fierce and aggressive people (cf. Jer 49:28–29). The prophet calls on all of these places and peoples to lift up praise for what God is accomplishing on behalf of those who endure the exile. For them God has transformed defeat into rescue, shame into awareness of God's personal and particular care for them. All of creation is called to respond to what they see and hear about—the deliverance of the people of Judah. This text recalls an earlier passage in Isaiah that speaks profoundly to the same situation: the people who dwelt in darkness and gloom have now seen a great light; for those who lived in a land of gloom, a light has risen (Isa 9:1).

The Lord makes himself known as a warrior who comes to announce what is in store for those who would fight against his people. Through the movement of salvation history, darkness and light have contended at the heart of the nation. The darkness of conquests suffered by Judah has been brought forth by the very hand of Almighty God, but it is the same Divine Warrior who proves to be the defender of the people, who now announce that the LORD will in person be their champion over their conquerors. The words present an image of God writhing in pain for the people as if laboring to give rebirth to a generation reduced to dust. For a time, God has remained silent, but now the moment has come for God to accomplish their redemption, once promised and now to be fulfilled.

The prophet draws on two images throughout his pronouncements: blindness and knowledge. These are especially highlighted in the prophetic calling in Isaiah 6: when God leads the blind on a road they did not know, this refers to a people who had been unobservant of God's ways, blinded by a lack of knowledge of God's expectations. Now God gives them the knowledge and insight to see and understand what will be accomplished for the people formed by his own deeds: God will give them another chance. It will indeed be a second exodus, a movement out of captivity and into freedom, out of blindness to God's law and into the light of God's vision for these claimed as the Lord's own. It is important to note in vv. 14–16 that it is God who speaks. It is a declaration of salvation and redemption. What God has promised is now being accomplished; the light of divine revelation now shines forth.

In our world today, we see and hear of many people who live under oppression, exiled from their homelands, and denied the dignities that are the right of each human being. As we pray from the text of this canticle, we are reminded of our own world, of cries that arise demanding our prayerful remembrance of so many in need of help and support. On a very personal level, each of us knows the weaknesses and sinfulness that continue to bind us in our daily lives. Whether self-imposed or forced on us by others, we pray that we may be freed from bondage so as to be able to "sing to the Lord a new song," who wills our freedom and promises to accomplish it, to deliver us and enable us to discern a way forward, often by "a road we do not know." But that is how God saves and redeems us, pouring out divine grace and leading us, quietly and mysteriously, into freedom and new life.

Isaiah 42:10–16

10 Sing to the LORD a new song,
his praise from the ends of the earth—
you who go down into the sea, and its fullness,
the islands and those who dwell there.

11 Let the desert and its cities exult,
the villages where Kedar dwells.
Let the inhabitants of Sela shout for joy;
let them sing from the tops of the mountains.
12 Let them give glory to the LORD,
and announce his praise in the islands.

13 The LORD strides forth like a champion,
like a warrior he rouses his rage;
he raises his voice and shouts aloud,
he shows his might against his foes.

14 I have always kept silent,
kept quiet, restraining myself.
Now I cry out like a woman in labor;
I both gasp and pant.

15 Mountains and hills will I lay waste;
and all their plants will I wither.
And rivers will I turn into islands,
and cause the marshes to dry up.

[16] I will lead the blind by a road they do not know;
and on paths they do not know I will lead them.
I will turn darkness into light before them,
and rough places into level ground.

Canticle Prayer

Lord of deliverance and God of redemption, who work the wonder of salvation in our world even today, we acknowledge the bonds that continue to hold us captive. Free us by the power of your grace, so that we may come to recognize your compassion and mercy in our lives, always acknowledging your power and might within us. Through Christ our Lord.

TUESDAY

Daniel 3:26–27, 29, 34–41

For the Sake of Your Name

It is particularly important to understand the larger context of this canticle in order to appreciate its message. Those who pray the Liturgy of the Hours will find each Sunday at the office of Lauds, or Morning Prayer, segments of the Canticle of the Three Young Men in the fiery furnace. Those songs are translations from the version of the Book of Daniel as it appears in the Greek version of the Hebrew Scriptures commonly referred to as the Septuagint. This canticle designated for Tuesday morning is actually the opening text of those Sunday canticles from the same source (Dan 3:52–88a). Yet this portion is quite different in character from the other two. While the later portions praise God for various elements of creation, Tuesday's text from the same canticle is more properly identified as a communal lament and confession of wrongdoing. Though a communal lament, the prayer is attributed to Azariah alone. Azariah is one of the three young men who have been cast into the furnace for having refused the command of the Babylonian king Nebuchadnezzar that they offer homage to a golden statue—an idol; and Azariah's words are delivered from within the fiery furnace. Though interpretations of who or what this statue represents are varied and numerous, the importance for us is to understand that the Babylonian authorities have imposed an act of idolatry on the faithful Judahites, who refuse to comply because the Mosaic law commands that they worship only the LORD of the covenant. The sentence of death is to be carried out by throwing them into this fiery furnace, but the attempted execution fails; the fire does not consume them, and they are presented with prayers of praise and gratitude on their lips.

The prayer offered in this text begins with an expression of praise of God's worthiness of praise, worthiness founded on divine justice. The prayer then acknowledges Israel's transgression against the covenant relationship. The language is notably strong from two perspectives: confessing the depth of their shared sinfulness ("we have failed in everything"), yet calling for divine compassion and forgiveness ("do not abandon us...whom you promised to multiply...as the stars of heaven"). Azariah recalls the very beginnings of God's relationship with Abraham and his descendants, emphasizing how God's fidelity through history comes to this very moment of trial and even martyrdom. At the same time, it sounds as though the people have finally grasped in Azariah's words the depth of their longstanding sinfulness. Yet they further recognize that they have only one hope: divine mercy, an expectation based on the initial promise to their ancestors. They find themselves humbled before all the nations because of their infidelity to God's goodness. Their captivity in Babylon is not unreasonable; their initial covenant with God expressly affirmed that God would remain faithful as long as the people on their part did the same. In v. 25, the word *transgression* bears the nuance of sin that is especially deplorable: the people knew the wrongness of their purposes, understood in their hearts the gravity of such intentions, but acted upon them anyway. It is a profound expression of the people's disloyalty and betrayal of their relationship with God.

Now in exile, the people see and recognize that they have brought all this suffering and torment upon themselves. They have created the miserable state in which they find themselves—having been idolatrous and unfaithful to the law, and now subject to punishment for their deeper betrayal of God's love and compassion. They are reduced to a point where they have no claim to God's mercy; and yet they know that only the divine gift can now save them. Through Azariah's words, they cry out in confession of all they have lost because of their sins: they have no spiritual leader, no opportunity for authentic worship, and no ability to present the fruits that represent their meager efforts to be faithful. Yet they continue to hope that God will comprehend their broken and contrite hearts as a true interior sacrifice manifesting conversion and hope for the return of God's friendship and acceptance.

The final lines of the canticle speak of interior sacrifice of the heart that is expressed as conversion—their wholehearted search for God. They are ready to commit themselves to abide by God's law unswervingly. These words anticipate Jesus's own invitation to follow after him unreservedly in seeking God's face. Jesus himself explains that following him makes radical demands—conversion of heart and change of life. Yet the path thus followed leads to union with God and eternal life. Consider these texts from the New Testament, where we find in the Gospels these words on the lips of Jesus: "Whoever loves father or mother more than me is not worthy of me"; "Whoever does not take up his cross and follow after me is not worthy of me. Whoever finds his life will lose it, and whoever loses his life for my sake will find it" (Matt 10:37–39; see also Luke 9:24; 14:26–27; Mark 8:35; John 12:25). With this canticle from Daniel we confess our wayward human existence and are invited to seek the face of God. We discover in such reassessment how our own lives can move from an acknowledgment of wrongdoing to an authentic change of heart.

Daniel 3:26–27, 29, 34–41

26 Blessed are you, O Lord, God of our ancestors,
worthy of praise, and glorious forever is your name.
27 For you are just in all you have done for us.

29 Indeed, we have sinned and transgressed
by departing from you;
we have failed in everything.

34 For the sake of your name, do not abandon us forever,
nor annul your covenant;
35 do not withdraw your mercy from us,
for the sake of Abraham your beloved,
Isaac your servant, and Israel your holy one,
36 to whom you promised to multiply their offspring
as the stars of heaven and the sand on the seashore.

37 For we are reduced beyond any other nation,
and in all the world we are humbled this day,
O Lord, on account of our sins.

38 And in our day, there is no prince, or prophet, or leader,
no holocaust, sacrifice, oblation, or incense,
no place to offer first fruits before you and find mercy.

39 But with contrite soul and humble spirit
may we be accepted,

as though with holocausts of rams and bulls,
or tens of thousands of fattened lambs.

40 So may our sacrifice be in your presence today,
as we follow you wholeheartedly;
for those who trust in you will not be put to shame.
41 And now we follow you with all our heart;
we fear you and we seek your face.

Canticle Prayer

God of mercy and Lord of compassion, who have yourself experienced the struggles we face in the midst of our life's journey: strengthen us to know that by acknowledging our sinfulness and turning to you we may a find path to a true conversion of heart. Grant us the vision of delight that comes in seeking, experiencing, and knowing your holy presence and welcoming countenance. Through Christ our Lord.

WEDNESDAY

Isaiah 61:10–11; 62:1–5

Builder and Bridegroom

Today's canticle belongs to the final section of the Book of Isaiah, chapters 56–66, sometimes referred to as Third Isaiah or Trito-Isaiah; this jubilant text is located in the midst of this extended passage. As a preface to subsequent passages, chapters 60–62 provide words of hope and promise of blessing that ameliorate the judgments and oracles of complaint that follow. Jerusalem had been destroyed in 587 BCE, its community taken into exile in Babylon; in 538 BCE, a group of Jews is released from captivity and allowed to return to Jerusalem; only a small number chose to do so. Most of Third Isaiah is produced during this time of struggle to rebuild both the temple and the community of Jerusalem itself. The speaker of this canticle is the prophet who offers God's promise of a forthcoming epiphany, attended by divine revitalization, deliverance, and redemption for the small and struggling community of returnees. The language and imagery of this section are consonant with earlier parts of the Book of Isaiah, where judgment has been passed on earlier infidelity. In Isaiah 40—55, an invitation to return to the land is proffered, replete with visions of God's loving compassion for the people who accept the invitation. God's judgment having passed, Third Isaiah holds out great hope—hope that Zion's inhabitants will now follow in God's ways. Fidelity to divine commands will bring blessings and renewal for those who are faithful to God's word and worship.

Read together, these verses bring forward a compendium of images from the Old Testament prophets that points to a new future, a forthcoming act of divine deliverance that will far exceed human expectation. Yet these people, repatriated and resettling the land, know that God has accomplished this before in the history of the chosen people. Once slaves in Egypt, they were liberated so as to enter a new land and find there a new identity. The prophet is here telling them that this oracle announces a new exodus, where God again acts as their Divine Deliverer. The earlier prophets employed all the imagery found here, imagery that fills out ancient oracles of new life and vitality, oracles now heard again: a royal wedding (54:6; 61:10; 62:3, 5), garments of salvation (61:10), vegetation and growth (61:11), nations in awe (62:2), a new name (62:4), a blessed land (62:4), and divine delight (61:4, 5). The cumulative effect of these images portrays a determined God who will be faithful in restoring what was lost: a new identity granted, a marriage covenant renewed, a rebuilt Jerusalem/Zion, and restored possession of the land upon which their dignity before the nations is reestablished. Underlying this whole canticle is faith in God's act of pure and unmerited grace, manifesting divine delight in those whom He once brought into being and continues to sustain.

In exile, the people of Judah had been stripped of all that marked them out as God's people. They were forced to live outside the land that God had given them. Their worship in the temple before the divine presence on Mount Zion was only a dream of the past. They were looked upon by other nations as a people without home or identity, a people abandoned by their divine protector. Once united to God in an everlasting covenant (Isa 55:3–4), they had broken this sacred bond, and captivity was the result. All the elements and images that bespoke their life in relation to God had disappeared; they would be renewed only if the people could again authentically embrace their relationship with God. Now the prophet is announcing to them a new identity in relation to God. And with that comes images of a relationship transformed, filled with images of blessing: garments of salvation as their clothing; vindication from former oppressors; a divine-human marriage symbolizing the covenant now rehabilitated and enhanced; and a new identity before the world.

A distinctive element of this canticle is the announcement of new names that will be given to the people who have returned to Judah and Jerusalem. From even the earliest histories recounted in the biblical text, we can see how important characters have received new names: Abram becomes Abraham, Sarai becomes Sarah, Jacob becomes Israel. All of these examples indicate that a change of identity accompanies a new name, giving them or their mission enhanced importance. Similarly, cities also receive symbolic names, providing insight into their new identity or way of living. Earlier in the Book of Isaiah, it is told that the city of Jerusalem, having renounced evil, will be called "city of justice" and "faithful city" (Isa 1:26). In Third Isaiah these new names are themselves descriptive changes in character and way of life. The same movement from infidelity to faithfulness that marked that earlier passage now demonstrates the action of God's grace in the hearts of the people as the Lord alters and adds to the names of Jerusalem and Zion. Having been considered a people forsaken by their God, they will now be known as God's own delight (61:4). Similarly, the land of Judah, once known for being desolate and alone, will again be seen as espoused to the God who welcomes them back and rejoices in them.

Today we live in a world quite different from the postexilic situation of the Book of Isaiah. Yet the images used by the prophet can speak with words of hope to our own situations and experiences. We too look upon disasters such as wars, situations of political conflict, uprisings, revolts, insurrections—conditions that tragically increase human suffering and anguish. We behold environmental disasters originating in nature itself or in human disregard for nature. Such experiences affect our world in concrete ways: they demand attention and action from anyone who sees the suffering they cause; they raise a desire to act so as to help relieve the level of pain and sorrow that too many people must bear. Often, we feel helpless before such implacable events. Only with the faith and trust that allows us to reach into the realm of God's grace can we hope that our prayer will be heard and attended to by our compassionate God, who brings life out of death, justice out of wrong, and hope out of despair. This hope-filled canticle invites us to consider to what depths human sinfulness can bring us, and only then to be led to realize God's profound gifts of redemption, forgiveness, and vindication. Such canticles lead us first to look at our need for redemption, and then to rejoice in the limitless mercy of God that the prophet's vision helps us realize.

Isaiah 61:10–11; 62:1–5

61:10 I will greatly rejoice in the Lord,
and my soul shall exult in my God;
for he has clothed me in the garments of salvation,

and wrapped me in the robe of saving justice,
like a bridegroom adorned with a crown,
and like a bride bedecked with her jewels.

11 For as the earth brings forth its growth,
and a garden makes what is sown in it sprout up,
so the Lord GOD will make righteousness and praise
sprout up in the sight of all the nations.

62:1 For Zion's sake I will not keep silent,
for Jerusalem's sake I will not keep still,
until her vindication shines forth like the dawn,
and her salvation like a flaming torch.

2 Nations shall behold your vindication,
and every king your glory;
and you shall be called by a new name
which the mouth of the LORD shall declare.

3 You shall be a crown of beauty
in the hand of the LORD,
and in the hand of your God a royal diadem.

4 No more shall you be called "Forsaken,"
nor your land be called "Desolate."
But you shall be called "My Delight is in her,"
and your land "Espoused."
For the LORD delights in you,
and your land shall be espoused.

5 For as a young man marries a virgin
your Builder shall marry you;
and as a bridegroom rejoices in his bride,
so will your God rejoice in you.

Canticle Prayer

God of infinite mercy and compassion, who hear our prayer and know our desperate need: Open our hearts to share in the suffering of others by remembering them often in our prayer, and lead us to give of ourselves in whatever ways we can, even in the simplest acts of kindness and care. Through Christ our Lord.

THURSDAY

Isaiah 66:10–14a

Mother Jerusalem

This canticle holds a special place in the Book of Isaiah as part of its final chapter. Scholarship of the last 150 years concludes that this book, the first of the major prophets, was composed in three distinct periods of biblical history: broadly understood, chapters 1–39 of Isaiah derive from the preexilic period, chapters 40–55 from the exilic period, and chapters 56–66 from the postexilic period. In studying the Book of Isaiah it is important to understand how it came together over its long history of composition, and what message the final redactor(s) intended. What meaning does the Book of Isaiah seek to impress upon its readers? In examining it from beginning to end, we find textual clues in each of the three divisions, passages repeated throughout the book that give a sense of unity to the whole corpus. Most scholars accept that the sixty-six chapters were not composed by a single author. But those who worked to compile its oracles and narratives—probably including disciples of the prophet himself—recognized and incorporated connections between the three distinct parts of the text to form and fashion its unity. To understand this challenging concept, one must be open to understanding and appreciating a rhetorical style in Hebraic poetry that is quite unlike styles of poetic composition employed today. Themes introduced in chapter 6—the prophet's inaugural vision and call—recur throughout the book. Identifying its origins in an oral culture will have a significant impact on one's understanding and appreciation of its style. This reiteration and repetition of key words and images establishes a remarkable continuity of theme and message that unifies the Book of Isaiah.

In any good contemporary novel, an author makes every effort to construct a well developed plot and eventually bring it to a satisfying conclusion. The same method is essential to biblical Hebraic narrative and poetry. In this short passage we can see an example of how this is accomplished. Textual analysis observes that the biblical author or redactor here brings together key themes from throughout the book, highlighting them for the reader. Let us look specifically at the motifs of Mother Jerusalem, the nations, and divine comfort as they appear in this canticle.

We cannot overestimate the significance of the city of Jerusalem to the biblical world. It was understood to be the place of God's dwelling among the children of Israel. It was where David entered into covenant with God on behalf of those who had come to know themselves as the chosen people. Yet in the very first chapter, the prophet judges this people in harsh and unflattering terms: "The faithful city, so upright, has become a prostitute" (v. 21). Yet before the chapter ends, the prophet comes to foretell that "Zion shall be redeemed by justice, and her repentant ones by righteousness" (v. 27). A purification of the people must come about—an event to be brought about by God, but including a choice on the people's part to live uprightly and honestly. For this canticle, the prophecy has come to pass for Jerusalem; the covenant has been renewed. Those who once mourned over her now see her as a loving nursing mother, consoling the children who once endured exile for their wayward conduct, but who now rejoice. This happy state is the effect of conversion, of their having found the way back to the One God who had long ago given them the land where they could worship freely and faithfully. "See, I am creating new heavens and a new earth; the former things shall not be remembered nor come to mind....I am creating Jerusalem to be joy and its people a delight" (Isa 65:17–18).

The nations who saw Judah and Israel exiled in shame now see the divine blessings that have returned to her. In Isaiah 60, Judah lies prostrate on the ground when the light of divine glory comes to shine upon her. The nations are drawn toward this light; they come to behold what God has done for Judah. God's glory is now bestowed upon her whom the nations ridiculed and despised. She who was thought to be forsaken and abandoned now stands as God's bride, in whom the Lord delights (Isa 62:4–5). The wealth and possessions of the nations will come to be her own (Isa 60:5–9; 66:12); it is a scene in which Jerusalem enjoys divine abundance, and the nations can only stand in awe before God's redemptive act on Israel's behalf.

In this movement out of exile and back to the land, the prophet uses the word *comfort* with deliberate significance. Isaiah 40 begins with a repeated instance of the imperative verb, where the prophet commands the heavenly court with divine authorization: "Comfort, give comfort to my people, says your God." After the double humiliation of exile and defeat, the prophet calls God's holy attendants to bring to the people—still exiled in Babylon—both a word of comfort and the announcement that God will renew the broken covenant. God had formerly declared, "*You* shall be *my people*, and *I* will be *your God*" (cf. Gen 17:7, Exod 6:7); in the opening words of this passage, the prophet now repeats, *my people...your God*. The declaration signals that the broken relationship is now to be renewed. The comfort that news brings is sustained to the end of this book. In v. 13, Isaiah brings together the image of Mother Jerusalem and the comfort she brings to her children. This image of maternal comfort arises in the context of a whole chapter telling of God's free and gratuitous gift of love, the renewal of the covenant, and the reestablishment of Jerusalem—the place of divine Presence. It is important to note here that the author uses a feminine image of God, a loving and comforting mother who gives nourishment to her once-lost children, now found and restored to her.

It is difficult to parse out all that can well up from this brief canticle for those who pray it in its biblical context. It brings the richest hopes of the prophet to fulfillment and more. It declares that God's loving care for his people knows no bounds. It brings an end to shame and to recriminations of unfaithfulness—parts of Judah's past, now to be forgotten forever, overtaken by healing, by memories of past joy renewed and made present again. God takes up all the pains and sorrows that have long burdened the people and threatened their very life—and entirely forgives them. Such forgiveness is a true reminder of the unboundedness of God's mercy and compassion. For us, this profound sense of God's love may recall occasions when we experience gracious acts of forgiveness shown to us. Even more, it invites us to acknowledge the pain we may have brought to others, intentionally or unintentionally, and thus to share as well in the mercy God shows toward those whom we have hurt.

Isaiah 66:10–14a

10 Rejoice with Jerusalem, exult in her,
all you who love her.
Rejoice with her in joy,
all who were mourning over her,

11 so that you may nurse and be satisfied
from her consoling breast,
so that you may drink deeply and delight
in the abundance of her glory.

12 For thus says the LORD: "Behold, I will extend to her
peace like a river, and the glory of the nations
like a stream in full flood.
You will be suckled, carried on the hip,
and gently bounced on her knees.

13 As a mother comforts her son,
so I will comfort you,
and in Jerusalem you shall find comfort.

14 You shall see and your heart shall rejoice;
your limbs shall flourish like grass."

Canticle Prayer

God of infinite compassion, enable us to see and appreciate the many ways in which you have renewed us through forgiveness. Strengthen us in this experience to act as you do, with all the mercy and forgiveness toward others that is possible to our limited human state. May we become true bearers of your Son Jesus, who dwells within us through the Holy Spirit, forever and ever.

FRIDAY

Tobit 13:1b–6

A Bright Light

In the first week of the Liturgy of the Hours, Tuesday at Lauds brings us the opening eight verses of a long prayer from Tobit. Today, in this final week of the Liturgy of the Hours, we have a decoupage of verses taken from the conclusion of the same prayer. We recall the story behind the Book of Tobit: Tobit, strangely blinded, sends his son Tobiah to distant Media in search of his father's wealth; he is accompanied by an unknown guide (revealed to be the archangel Raphael), and there encounters Sarah, an unjustly cursed woman who later, amid jubilant celebration, becomes Tobiah's wife. The story illustrates the Deuteronomic theme that those who live God's law faithfully will, after trials, come to know divine favor in the end. Running through the whole narrative as a kind of quiet fugal theme is the providence of God, whose divine plan brings blessings to all the characters in the story. Much like Job, Tobit bears his suffering with patience, trusting in God throughout; he ultimately receives abundant blessing for his fidelity and wisdom.

"Then you will rejoice and exult," Tobit says (v. 13), for (if we may interpolate) you have shown yourself to be living the law of God with a mind that desires to serve God and obey the divine law. How important it is to notice the *then* in this context: the plan of God, manifest countless times in the Scriptures, can lead us on a circuitous route. Tobit buries a slain countryman, cares for orphans, feeds the hungry, and repudiates Gentile food, showing himself a true Israelite. But despite his regard for the law, he is struck with blindness and afflicted for many years. Even so, toward the end of Tobit's life, his son Tobiah secures a cure for Tobit's blindness. We may smile at the form the cure takes in the ancient story, recognizing it as medically absurd. But what is important to our understanding of the story is that the Deuteronomic principle of faithful behavior does indeed bring blessing and healing to God's devoted and trustworthy adherent. *Now* you face difficulties. But "*then* you will rejoice."

In our progress through the story, the unexpected arrival of a faithful companion for Tobiah's journey (5:2–6), the revelation of a cure for Sarah's curse (6:7–8), and the finding of an effective ointment for Tobit's blindness (6:9)—these events are totally unforeseen. The God who has brought all people and all things into existence continues to keep watch over them. Whether small or great, the lives of all are touched by God. The Psalmist writes,

"The LORD frustrates the designs of the nations; he defeats the plans of the peoples. The designs of the LORD stand forever, the plans of his heart from age to age" (33:10–11). The whole biblical story continually shows that God has a plan for the human family. A great mystery is at work when we discern the providential care of God in the lives of God's people through the biblical narrative—and it is just as certainly at work in our lives today. From a wider perspective, we know that God continues to provide for the care of creation, even as human creatures seem less and less concerned about their own impact on the world. Thus, our own concern for the environment, our care for the people of our world and all that is in it, our attention and watchfulness over all things and peoples—these attitudes ennoble us as emissaries of God to creation.

The two biblical figures of Tobit and Job stand side by side in terms of righteous living and personal misfortune. In the opening chapters of the Tobit, the title character is distinguished as one who knows what is upright, performing it with firm and energetic conviction. When he encounters a situation that must be rectified, he is moved in both mind and heart. He sees it as a call to action on behalf of justice, of righting what is wrong. The whole of chapter 4 takes on the form of a valediction to his son, the passing on of wisdom that has informed Tobit's own life and that he hopes will inform the life of his son. "My son, do what is upright…remain righteous in all your ways"—how often we encounter such counsel in the Book of Proverbs! The biblical world understood the importance of this passing on of wisdom, of the experience of a life that has been well lived. Tobit shows himself to be a man who knows well the challenges of life, the pitfalls of human behavior, and the extent to which one's life can have an effect on others. It provides a valuable examination of conscience for any one of us. Though the Book of Tobit presents a somewhat fanciful story replete with colorful characters, it also expresses important truths for living life authentically before God and one another.

In v. 11, the image of a brilliant light may recall Isaiah 60—a high point in the prophet's word to a people returning to live in a place that had once been taken from them. Such transitions mark the lives of all humans: times when new beginnings show forth great grace, events that turn our lives in surprising directions. Looking for God's providence in these situations is not always easy, yet it remains an important undertaking. The Book of Tobit stretches us to see and find God in all times, places, and people—especially when our hopes are great, but the way to their fulfillment seems dark or doubtful. The example of Tobit's faith and trust continues to speak to us today.

Tobit 13:1b–6

[1b] Blessed be God, who lives forever,
and blessed be his kingdom,
[2] for he punishes but also shows mercy.

He leads down to the depths of Hades,
and brings up from ruin by his majesty;
and no one can escape his hand.

[3] Children of Israel, confess him before the nations,
for he has scattered you among them,
[4] and even there has shown you his greatness.

Extol him, then, before every living being,
for he is our Lord and our Father,
he is our God forever.

[5] He will punish you for your iniquities,
but on all of you he will have mercy,
he will gather you from all the nations
wherever you have been scattered.

[6] When you turn back to him
with all your heart and all your soul
to do what is true before him,
then he will turn back to you
and no longer hide his face from you.

Now, then, see what he has done for you,
and with full voice, give him your thanks.

Canticle Prayer

God our Creator, Lord of history, who time and again bring us back to the ways of wisdom: give us courage to proceed on your path. Strengthen our meager efforts to do justice, love goodness, and walk humbly with you (Mic 6:8). We affirm your constant presence, knowing you are closer to our situations than we can comprehend. Grant us eyes to see with faith, ears to hear with trust, and feet to walk with courage in the ways you show us, through Christ our Lord.

SATURDAY

Ezekiel 36:24–28

A New Heart

In contemporary language, we might say that this passage speaks of God performing a divine transplant of the human heart, along with the giving of a new spirit. While reading this short canticle, delivered to the people in exile, what we should keep in mind is that it is perhaps best understood in terms of significant contrasts. Responding to vv. 25 and 26, we might well ask, "Why do the people need a new heart, or a new spirit? And why does God need to purify them?" The Book of Ezekiel opens with the prophet held captive, a man in exile near the rivers of Babylon. The exile is, as the people understand it, a punishment from God for their infidelity, idolatry, and disregard for the covenant precepts. God has passed judgment, and much of the prophecy recounts what the people have done to break the covenant and incur this judgment. But as the message of their betrayal unfolds, the sense of condemnation eventually gives way to hope that God has plans to renew—or even better, to recreate, reestablish, and restore what has been shattered and squandered. The movement is one of strong contrasts: from infidelity to fidelity, from impurity to purity, from profanation to integrity of worship. Israel has shown it can never accomplish such a restoration by its own resources: it will be only through God's power and love that this will be achieved.

In the verses immediately preceding this canticle, God, speaking through the prophet, reveals to Israel the divine plan to reverse the judgment and punishment. God does so not primarily for the well-being of the people, but rather for the glory of God's own holy name. In the context of Hebraic biblical culture, one's name was understood as identified with one's power, stature, and identity. Once the deed is accomplished, the nations will see and know the divine power of the Lord GOD. Only by such significant and overwhelming acts of God's Spirit can the nations comprehend the divine will to restore and manifest the love of the covenant. God will manifest an identity that is faithful and loving to Israel. In returning them to the land of their origins, God accomplishes a second exodus, a new and wondrous liberation for a new generation of God's covenant people.

The lesson for Israel must include the fact that their life as a nation is marked by infidelity. They have been incapable of living in relationship with God, as they had once promised in the covenant. Rather, their idolatry has continued for generations. As a consequence, they must first be purified and made clean in a symbolic ritual that purges their iniquities. Three times in a single verse (Ezek 36:25) the text speaks of cleansing: "I will sprinkle *clean* water...you shall be *cleansed*...of your idols, I will *cleanse* you." Once the people are cleansed of their past, God can begin the process of recreation, regeneration, and restoration. The people are described as being rebellious in their relationship with God from early times; their betrayals have hardened their hearts (Ps 95:8; Isa 63:17; Heb 3:8, 15; 4:7), rendering them incapable of conversion and renewal. There is a sense that God must rescue the people from themselves, by implanting within them hearts of flesh. Only by such an act of divine love, such a sign of God's holiness, can this great thing be accomplished.

"You shall dwell in the land I gave your ancestors" (v. 28). To the biblical mindset, the land means the place God had once given Israel where they were to worship him in truth and fidelity. They had been taken from Egypt, a land of idolatry and slavery, then tested in the desert, and finally brought into the land where they could worship God as his chosen people. By that first rescue, God showed the nations both his power and his love for Israel. Now in the time of Ezekiel, the people would once again be brought back to their land, that place once given them in love where they could live in fidelity toward God. God had done this once before and was now about to do it again so that the nations would again know that the Lord GOD expresses his holy name—his identity and power—for all to behold in wonder.

With this text, the Old Testament canticles of the Office of Lauds or Morning Prayer are brought to completion. The message of the entire cycle attests to the ongoing recreation of the world by God—and perhaps more significantly, to the recreation and renewal of each of us. As children of God, we are cared for by a Creator and Father who has been with us since our entry into the world—our conception, our birth, our deification in the waters of baptism, and our renewal by sharing in the sacred mysteries of the Church. We can never fully grasp the grace of God that surrounds and fills us in the things of creation, yet the moments of reawakening to the mystery of divine love continue to mark our lives as children of God, blessed beyond measure.

Ezekiel 36:24–28

24 I will take you from the nations,
and gather you from all the lands,
and bring you onto your own soil.

25 Then I will sprinkle clean water on you;
you shall be cleansed of all your impurity
and of all your idols I will cleanse you.

26 And I will give you a new heart,
and a new spirit I will place within you.
I will remove the heart of stone from your flesh,
and I will give you a heart of flesh.

27 I will place my Spirit within you
and make you walk according to my statutes;
and my judgments you shall keep and observe.

28 Then you shall dwell in the land I gave your ancestors,
and you shall be my people, and I will be your God.

Canticle Prayer

O God, our Savior, Redeemer, and Deliverer, who walk with your people through the dark valleys and the spacious plains of our life, we thank you for your daily guidance and encouragement. Continue to lead us in the paths of justice and peace as we walk with a heart and spirit that are renewed by your grace and goodness, your compassion and generosity. We praise you for your boundless gifts, through Christ our Lord.

II

CANTICLES FOR EVENING PRAYER

SUNDAY 1 / SATURDAY EVENING

Philippians 2:6–11

Christ Emptied Himself

THE CANTICLE FROM Paul's Letter to the Philippians holds an honored place in the Liturgy of the Hours. Each Saturday evening at Vespers, as we enter into the Sunday celebration of the Lord's resurrection, this canticle announces the motif of the great paschal mystery. Each Sunday our commemoration of the passion, death, and resurrection of Christ recalls the mystery of this First of Days. Throughout the history of the Church, Sunday has been referred to as a "little Easter," recapitulating with each new week the heart of our Christian faith. In this vein it is also worth noting that the canticle is used as the reading at Mass for the Feast of the Exaltation of the Holy Cross (September 14). The canticle reminds us that the Father has fully accepted the total self-offering of Jesus, and has brought him to glory and exaltation by his resurrection. Psalm 118 (117), a psalm historically associated with the paschal mystery, appears in the Liturgy of the Hours each Sunday as well, proclaimed either at Lauds (Weeks 2 and 4) or Day Prayer (Weeks 1 and 3). In keeping with the canticle from Philippians, the psalm reminds us that "this is the day the Lord has made; let us rejoice in it and be glad" (v. 24). It goes on to say, "The stone that the builders rejected has become the cornerstone" (v. 22). These psalms were of course composed long before the Christian era, yet they resonate nonetheless with the theme of the paschal mystery, fulfilled in the person of Jesus Christ.

The canticle tells us that Christ "emptied himself" (v. 7). This declaration emphasizes the personal self-surrender of Jesus to the plan of God. In other words, Jesus was disposed and ready to accept the will of God for the salvation of the world, ready to accomplish this by paying the requisite price—his very life. The canticle expresses this by means of a supreme contrast: although in his divine nature Jesus possessed the very form of God (v. 6a), he willingly took on the form of a human being—a slave (v. 7b). The One who was wholly divine chose to become fully human. In doctrinal terms, this is called *kenotic* theology: it derives from the Greek word *kenosis*, which means "emptying, purging." What is so important for us to see and understand in this canticle is the consequence of God having chosen to be one of us—healing, redeeming, and saving us in our own nature—from inside to out, as it were. Never losing his divine status, his equality with God, Jesus took on the life of a human slave. In his doing so, the world comes to see the depths of God's love for the human race. He gave all so that we might receive all! The canticle reflects the theology and spirituality found in that passage from the Book of the prophet Isaiah (52:13—53:12) called the Fourth Song of the Servant of the LORD. There we read, "It was our pain he bore, our sufferings he endured...he bore the punishment that makes us whole, by his wounds we are healed" (vv. 4a, 5b). The call to self-surrender touches our lives in many ways—perhaps less dramatically than that of the Suffering Servant, but nonetheless challenging and often painful. Here, Jesus is the Teacher par excellence, guiding and directing us on the path to glory by both word and example.

Saint Paul's emphasis here on the obedience of Jesus lays out for our consideration a profound reality. *Obedire* or *obaudire*—the Latin root of the English word *obedience*—bears the sense of listening (*audire*), of paying attention, and even in some senses the responsibility of carrying out one's duty. What is important for our own reflection on the obedience of Jesus is the level of communion to which obedience can bring us—a communion that certainly existed between Jesus and his Father. The words of Jesus in the Garden of Gethsemane present to us a heartfelt prayer, an expression of communion between Father and Son: "My Father, if it is possible, let this cup pass from me; yet not as I will, but as you will" (Matt 26:39b). It can be helpful to think about obedience from two perspectives: with a lowercase *o* on a smaller, human level, and also with an uppercase O with respect to divine agency. When it is God who speaks, when there is an interior recognition of a duty, a call to fulfill a mission, *Obedience* takes on a special character. Its fulfillment possesses a sacred character in our life, even when it is in relationship with someone of equal standing. Here we see how Obedience shatters the doors of hell and opens the gates of paradise, as often depicted in both Greek and Russian icons of the resurrection.

The movement of the canticle attains its pinnacle as it speaks of the conferral of a *name* on Jesus: "God highly exalted [Jesus] and bestowed upon him the *name* that is above every other name" (v. 9). The word *name* is repeated three times in these later verses. We know that in the biblical tradition the change of a name implies a mission, a new identity—a new direction in life. We think of Abram becoming Abraham, Jacob becoming Israel, or Simon becoming Cephas (or Peter) as examples. A person's name can provide insight into their vision: it has associations with their mission, their self-identity—indeed, with their very life. God reveals the divine name *Yahweh* in Exodus 3:14: this name is usually translated as "I am who I am," but sometimes rendered as "I am who I will be." It expresses for human understanding the divine idea that "I am the God of all being, of all life, of all that is," identifying by name the God revealed at Sinai in the Hebrew Scriptures. To emphasize the holiness of this divine name, the four Hebrew letters of *Yahweh* came to be transcribed as "LORD," written thus in small capitals. The movement of the text to its end, then, declares "that Jesus Christ is Lord to the glory of God the Father" (v. 11bc). The name bestowed upon Jesus Christ is the same as God's: that is, "Lord." It is *not* to be understood as implying that Jesus had lost his divinity and then recovered it. Rather, when Saint Paul echoes the text of Isaiah 45:23b–24a ("'To me, every knee shall bend; to me every tongue shall swear, saying, 'Only in the Lord are just deeds and power'"), his statement resonates with the prophet's definition of divine might and asserts that this exaltation and greatness rightly belong to Christ, the divine One now risen and glorious. Paul's description of this salvific act—the act by which Christ lived the paschal mystery in a radical and redemptive way—confesses and professes the faith we place in Jesus Christ as believing Christians.

How often we encounter the word *name* in association with God: "Blest be the name of the Lord"; "Our help is in the name of the Lord"; Our Father...hallowed be thy name"; "We saw a man using your name to expel demons"; "In the name of Jesus Christ the Nazorean, rise and walk"; "Whoever calls on the name of the Lord will be saved." Again, we note that God reveals the divine name in Exodus 3:14 and provides for us the sense of an identity that we may apply to the mystery of God. At the same time, various expressions of the divine name help us to find our own connection with the God of life. Whether as redeemer, savior, teacher, Lord, Christ—whatever may arise in our heart to lead us to prayer—the names given to God in the Scriptures and in our lives become a way of personal union with our Creator and Lord. Saint Paul's proclamation of faith in Christ in the canticle from Philippians encourages us to do the same with trust, hope, and love.

Philippians 2:6–11

6 Although he was in the form of God,
Christ Jesus did not regard equality with God
something to be grasped.

7 Rather he emptied himself,
taking on the form of a slave
being born in human likeness;

and found to be in human form,
8 he humbled himself,
becoming obedient unto death,
death upon a cross.

9 And for this, God highly exalted him,
and bestowed upon him the name
that is above every other name.

10 So that at the name of Jesus
every knee shall bend
in the heavens, on the earth, and under the earth,

11 and every tongue confess
that Jesus Christ is Lord
to the glory of God the Father.

Canticle Prayer

O God, Creator and Father, Lord and Savior, who daily manifest yourself to us in the wonders of an ever-changing world: open our eyes to know the work of your hand and cleanse our ears to hear your loving voice. As we encounter the signs of your presence among us, lead us in the ways of gratitude, praise, intercession, and even lament, so that our communion with you will grow ever stronger. Through Christ, our risen and exalted Lord.

SUNDAY 2

Revelation 19:1–2, 5–7

The Wedding Feast of the Lamb

This canticle attains a more global sense of meaning for the praise and thanksgiving offered to God in the songs of Revelation. Again we see that the canticle is excised from a longer passage (Rev 19:1–7) with some contextual verses (vv. 3 and 4) omitted; the omitted verses are important for filling out the story of the people with whom this song of praise originates. The chapter prior to the canticle tells of the fall and destruction of Babylon, the biblical symbol of idolatry and depravity. In the Old Testament history of Israel, Babylon was the great power that invaded Jerusalem in 587 BCE; they destroyed the temple and took the people into captivity. After the Babylonian invasion, Jerusalem was left desolate. In the Book of Revelation, Babylon becomes the dwelling place of Satan and the Devil, where evil and sin are rampant; it is a place where depravity has held sway for centuries. Babylon is at last convicted of its long history of wickedness, of the shedding "of the blood of the prophets and of the holy ones slaughtered on earth" (Rev 18:24). This is the situation that leads into the opening verses of our canticle; it suggests that these Old Testament forebears of the Christians, people of faith and righteousness, are among the "great multitude in heaven" that proclaims, "Salvation and glory and power to our God" (Rev 19:1).

Progressing through vv. 3–4, the text moves from the saints and prophets of the Old Testament to those who have lived in the beginnings of the Christian era; this is made clear by the reference to those who participate in the wedding feast of the Lamb and his bride (v. 7), an explicitly Christian event. Then in v. 5, a voice comes from heaven, calling all the servants of God to praise their Lord. As vv. 1 and 2 refer to the pre-Christian prophets and holy ones, vv. 5 through 7 give us the praise and thanksgiving of those who have found and followed the Messiah, the Christ, the Anointed One; these have remained faithful and true to him through his life, death, and resurrection. We recall all the people in the New Testament writings—the Gospels, the Acts of the Apostles, the Pauline literature, and the Catholic Epistles; those about whom the stories tell and those to whom the stories are told—all those who adhered to Jesus's teaching, who repented of their disloyalties and failures and experienced his healing. This canticle brings together all who have sought God, those who awaited the coming of the Messiah, and those who now rejoice in his paschal victory and glory.

Verse 7 introduces us to the bride. Who is this bride? The full answer to this question is not found until the final two chapters of the Book of Revelation. "Then I saw a new heaven and a new earth. The former heaven and the former earth had passed away, and the sea was no more. I also saw the holy city, a new Jerusalem, coming down out of heaven, prepared as a bride adorned for her husband" (Rev 21:1–2). The bride of the Lamb is the Church, in all her splendor. By his paschal victory the Lamb has cleansed the city of Jerusalem of past sins and failures and made it new. It is a glorious vision of the end-times when God is all in all, and his bride, the Church, is dressed in the white robes of the righteous and redeemed (Rev 19:8).

cf. Revelation 19:1–2, 5–7

Alleluia!
1 Salvation and glory and power to our God,
(℟ Alleluia!)
2 for his judgments are true and just.
℟ Alleluia (alleluia).

Alleluia!
5 Sing praise to our God, all you his servants,

(℟ Alleluia!)
you who fear him, small and great.
℟ Alleluia (alleluia).

Alleluia!
6 For the Lord, our God the Almighty reigns.
(℟ Alleluia!)
7 Let us rejoice and exult, and give him the glory.
℟ Alleluia (alleluia).

Alleluia!
The marriage feast of the Lamb has come,
(℟ Alleluia!)
and his bride has prepared herself.
℟ Alleluia (alleluia).

Canticle Prayer

O God, whose grace is at work from the rising of the sun to its setting: establish among us your justice and truth, that we may see clearly the path you have set before us as the way to salvation. To you be all honor and glory forever.

MONDAY

Ephesians 1:3–10

Chosen in Christ

This canticle from the Letter to the Ephesians bears the characteristics of those psalms known as *hymns*: it offers up extravagant and elegant expressions of praise and thanksgiving for God's salvific act in Jesus Christ. In v. 9c, the canticle speaks of the plan established by God, who has set Christ as its center.

This plan is universal: it conveys the mystery of the divine will for the good of all people and of all time; as a mystery, it will unfold only as time progresses, and we are gradually brought into an awareness of what has been, gaining insight into what is actually happening in the world and in the life of each of us. When the sacred author includes "things in heaven, and things on earth" in this plan (v. 10c), the words express a cosmic dimension that we can only hope to comprehend with God's grace as our insight increases over time. This cosmic dimension suggests a vastness beyond the scope of ordinary human understanding. As such, our faith is called forth as a response; only belief, trust, and hope in God's will for our good can allow the divine mystery to take root in us. The promise of God expands the vision rising from belief; and while we must allow the mystery to remain ultimately beyond understanding, we must ponder these thoughts in our hearts, where God dwells and speaks to us, as the Scriptures tell us (cf. Rom 5:5; 8:9; 1 Cor 6:19; Eph 3:17; 1 John 2:27).

In this canticle Paul develops a number of topics in ways that deepen our understanding of God's mysterious plan. One key theme is the *election* of each person by God. The text tells us, "[God] has chosen us in [Christ]" (v. 4a). The notion of divine election is founded on the experience of the Hebrew slaves in Egypt, called forth from bondage to receive the promised land. Upon their arrival at Mount Sinai, God's tender words of care and support illustrate for them the meaning and measure of their election: "You have seen how I treated the Egyptians and how I bore you up on eagles wings and brought you to myself....You will be my treasured possession among all peoples, though all the earth is mine. You will be to me a kingdom of priests, a holy nation" (Exod 19:4–6). These words from Exodus, enunciating the initial encounter of the Hebrew people with the experience of divine election, come to have an eschatological meaning for us. What was once promised by God to the enslaved Hebrews has now come to fulfillment in Christ and in us: we are now among the elect, we are God's chosen ones. All that God had initially promised to the children of Abraham in bringing them out of Egypt has new and fuller meaning for us, because of Christ. What we experienced as God's redemption through the sacrificial blood of the lamb at the Passover we now know through the sacrificial blood of Christ poured out for us on the cross. "In [Christ] we have redemption through his blood, the forgiveness of transgressions" (Eph 1:7). From Exodus to Ephesians, we see that God's grace of election is freely given: gratuitous, pure gift, "lavished on us in all wisdom and insight" (v. 8). Through Christ's resurrection, our election, our adoption, comes through God's free and unmerited gift of grace. It has brought us freedom from sin and a promise of grace flowing to us through the risen life of Christ. Through Christ's blood, we belong to God as adopted and beloved children.

We are sometimes inclined to pass over words made familiar by frequent hearing or recitation, to our own spiritual loss. This is true for the canticle from Ephesians. The opening words, "Blessed be the God and Father of our Lord Jesus Christ" (v.3) are a resounding expression of praise, acclaim, and exaltation of the God who created the universe (the plural *heavens* in Greek), brought our world into being, and graciously redeemed us through his Son, Jesus Christ. The expression "God and Father of our Lord Jesus Christ" is distinct in the New Testament writings. It presents a clear connection between God and the Christ—the Father and the Son. It is *through* Christ that the Father has brought this blessing on the people of God. The canticle opens with reference to the fact of our being *in* Christ, which gives us reason to thank and bless God. The blessings of heavenly grace come to us who are in Christ, because of the merits of Christ's life, death, and resurrection. Here the sacred author highlights the great wisdom of God, poured out as grace and fulfilled by Jesus Christ, bringing all things together and recapitulating them in him. God is blest, praised, and exalted for this gracious love and faithfulness manifest in Christ—love and faithfulness that exist beyond words, yet allow our voices to ring out with profound gratitude.

Ephesians 1:3–10

3 Blessed be the God and Father of our Lord Jesus
Christ,
who has blessed us in Christ
with every spiritual blessing in the heavens;

4 just as he has chosen us in him
before the foundation of the world
to be holy and blameless before him in love.

5 He destined us for adoption
to himself through Jesus Christ,
in accord with the good pleasure of his will,
6 to the praise of his glorious grace,
with which he favored us in the Beloved.

7 In him we have redemption through his blood,
the forgiveness of transgressions,
in accord with the riches of his grace
8 lavished on us in all wisdom and insight.

9 He has made known to us the mystery of his will
in accord with his good pleasure,
which he set forth in Christ as a plan,
10 a plan for the fullness of times,
to recapitulate all things in him,
things in heaven, and things on earth.

Canticle Prayer

God of infinite wisdom and grace, whose wondrous plan of creation has given us adoption in Christ, grant us an ever-increasing knowledge of the election that manifests your goodness and favor in our lives, that we may praise you with ever deeper faith, hope, and trust. Through Christ our Lord.

TUESDAY

Revelation 4:11; 5:9b–10, 12b

Praise and Honor to the Creator of All and to the Slain Lamb

We may note that the text of this canticle comes from two chapters—4 and 5—of the Book of Revelation. That gives us some insight into the literary character of this and other canticles in the Book of Revelation. We infer from the surrounding text that these phrases are continually sung (Rev 4:11; 5:9); though noncontiguous, the phrases, when grouped together apart from the intervening text, appear to be fully developed canticles—acclamations of praise and thanksgiving. These colorful texts describe human weakness juxtaposed with divine judgment, underscoring God's victory in Christ for our salvation. These canticles are characterized as being sung before the heavenly throne. Seated on the throne is God the Father, and with him Jesus Christ, who is described in a variety of ways—a victorious Lamb, a slaughtered Lamb, the First and the Last and the Living One, God's Anointed, the Root and Offspring of David, the Firstborn of the dead, Ruler of the kings of the earth, King of kings and Lord of lords. Most recognizable is Jesus presented as the slain Lamb. This image of Jesus Christ as sacrificial lamb is drawn from Exodus 12 in the Old Testament, which speaks of the paschal lamb of the Passover meal. Christ, the slain lamb of the Book of Revelation, now "receives power and riches and wisdom, strength and honor, and glory and blessing"; the text intentionally reimagines the paschal lamb of Exodus that had inaugurated the freeing of the Hebrew slaves from their captivity in Egypt. Christ is now the paschal lamb who brings to all Christian believers deliverance from sin and death.

The significance of the lamb in the Book of Revelation is conveyed by the list of seven terms employed to describe Jesus's paschal sacrifice, a list that shapes our understanding of what has been accomplished through his death and resurrection. He has received "power and riches and wisdom, strength and honor, and glory and blessing." In biblical literature, the number seven represents perfection, completion, and totality. For the early Christians, especially those undergoing persecution, this would have been a message of hope, telling them that Christ, now in the heavenly realm, acts as the source and agent of salvation for those who, in the midst of struggle, put their trust in him. The blood of Christ has brought about the ransom of those united to him; they are the new people of God, drawn "from every tribe and tongue, and every people and nation" (Rev 7:9). The whole world has been delivered from the power of darkness and death, and ushered into the kingdom of light and hope.

These canticles appearing in the Book of Revelation form a kind of repertoire of the heavenly choir, made up of a varied group of people. The group includes the evangelists, symbolically presented as "the four living creatures" (4:6b–7), the twenty-four elders from among the holy ones (5:8), and the choirs of "many angels" (5:11). Each of the elders is "holding a harp and golden bowls full of incense, which are the prayers of the saints" (5:8b). The bowls of incense and prayers of the saints indicate that the scene is a heavenly liturgy at which the One seated on the throne and the Lamb are honored in an act of heavenly worship. The abundant symbols, taken from various sources in the Old Testament and reimagined for the New Testament, give us a deeper understanding that this new creation has been achieved through the passion, death, and resurrection of Christ. The canticles serve as acclamations to honor God upon his throne and Christ the Lamb whose death has altered the composition and direction of salvation history. The worthiness of those who are seated upon the throne—God as the author of salvation and his Christ, the slain Lamb—is affirmed three times in the text, which underscores the faith assertion that divine action has brought all of this to pass.

Revelation 4:11; 5:9b–10, 12b

4:11 Worthy are you, O Lord, our God
to receive glory and honor and power,
for you have created all things
and by your will they came to be and were created.

5:9b Worthy are you, O Lord, to receive the scroll
and to break open its seals,
for you were slain
and with your blood you have ransomed for God
those from every tribe and tongue,
and every people and nation:

10 And made them a kingdom and priests for our God,
and they shall reign on the earth.

12b Worthy is the Lamb that was slain
to receive power and riches and wisdom,
strength and honor, and glory and blessing.

Canticle Prayer

All holy and almighty God, dwelling in heavenly glory: hear the prayers of those who call to you in their need with the sure hope of your abundant goodness and mercy. Through Christ our Lord.

WEDNESDAY

Colossians 1:12–20

The Image of the Invisible God

The canticle from the Letter to Colossians is a kind of kaleidoscopic progression of revelation, presenting powerful images of the mystery of Christ's resurrection as it moves from verse to verse. Each verse—sometimes each individual line—expands our perception of the scope of God's great work of salvation through Jesus Christ. Christ is the beloved Son who ushers us from darkness to light; he is the Redeemer who has purchased forgiveness for us by his death on the cross. Christ is the firstborn of the new creation, in which we become his brothers and sisters. He makes visible for us the invisible God, whom we now behold in Christ even in this earthly existence. Christ's body now has its form in the Church, and as the head of this body, he has primacy over all created things; he is revealed now to everyone and everything as their origin and source. He has accomplished for this world, broken and burdened by sin, the reconciliation that reunites earth and heaven. Each of these progressive images builds up for the believing Christian a sense of the immeasurable impact of the power of God, unleashed in the resurrection of Jesus Christ. Our response of thanksgiving, limited as it is to merely human terms, can never reflect the full extent of God's plan for our deliverance as realized in Christ; yet the very words in which these images are couched make it possible for us to articulate our own belief in God's grand design for the salvation of the world.

The canticle lays out before us these marvelous images of what God has done for us. Yet the way of life that follows upon our recognition and acceptance of the good news of Christ's resurrection also necessarily places moral expectations on us, matters of justice and righteousness. What we find in the canticle draws forth our cooperation; we see that reconciliation is God's great vision for fallen creation and that we must become partners with Christ in bringing healing to a wounded and fragmented world. Reconciliation has been given to us as a gift that makes us coworkers with Christ. The world in which we live is still "coming to birth" in God's plan that is moving forward to fulfillment. When with Christ's light we come to see that sin lies within the very framework of our lives, it invites us to be lights ourselves, to become the instruments with which Christ shatters the darkness that burdens the world. We may call to mind Saint Paul's description of this reconciliation in the Second Letter to the Corinthians, and our partnership in it: "Whoever is in Christ is a new creation....All this is from God who has reconciled us to himself through Christ and given us the ministry of reconciliation....So we are ambassadors for Christ, as if God were appealing through us. We implore you on behalf of Christ, be reconciled to God" (5:17–20). As Christ served as God's representative and mediator, so we share in those same ministries in Christ wherever and whenever the opportunity arises. This is implicit in the rite of baptism, the initial call that declares how our lives are to witness those movements from darkness and sin into light and service of one another.

Saint Paul introduces the image of the Body of Christ in the Letter to the Romans: "We, though many, are one body in Christ" (12:5); he reiterates the image in the First Letter to the Corinthians: "We, though many, are one body" (10:17). And here in the canticle we are now considering, Paul develops this image of the Church further by emphasizing the particular relationship between Christ and each member of the Body. As Christ is "the head of the body" (v. 18), so there is a direct connection between him and each member of the body. This relationship is of course both a privilege and a duty. Once we have meditated upon the rich endowment that is ours in Christ's sacrificial death and resurrection, we immediately understand that we are being summoned to act. The inscrutable yet inevitable unfolding of

God's great gift beckons us to look into our lives and realize ever more fully the consequences of having been gifted in this awesome way. With the realization of the privilege, of how we have been blessed, there comes simultaneously the challenge to live the paschal mystery in ever new and fruitful ways.

Sometimes the smallest words take on a special importance. Consider the numerous times that prepositions occur in this canticle: "*in* whom we have redemption, the forgiveness of sins" (v. 14); "*in* him all things...were created....All were created *through* him and *for* him" (v. 16); "*in* him all things hold together" (v. 17b); "that he might have primacy *in* all things" (v. 19a) "for *in* him all the fullness was pleased to dwell" (v. 19b); "*in* him all things hold together" (v. 17b); "*through* him, to reconcile all things to himself" (v. 20a); "both those on earth and those *in* the heavens" (v. 20b); "making peace *through* the blood of his cross" (v. 20c). Prepositions show *relationship*: from a theological perspective, these numerous prepositions help us to see how Christ is the center point of God's plan for redemption. From a spiritual perspective, we see the close relationship that unites us—as human beings, as children of God, as brothers and sisters of Christ—to the one great Source of our prayer: to Him who is the inspiration for our reflection, the cause of our hope, and spring of our future glory.

cf. Colossians 1:12–20

12 Let us give thanks to the Father who has made us worthy
to share the heritage of the holy ones in light.

13 He delivered us from the power of darkness
and transferred us to the kingdom of his beloved Son,
14 in whom we have redemption, the forgiveness of sins.

15 He is the image of the invisible God,
the firstborn of all creation,
16 for in him all things in heaven and on earth were
created,
things visible and invisible,
whether thrones or dominions, principalities or
powers.

All were created through him and for him,
17 and he exists before all things,
and in him all things hold together.

18 He is the head of the body, the Church,
the beginning, the firstborn from the dead
19 that he may have primacy in all things.

For in him all the fullness was pleased to dwell,
20 and through him, to reconcile all things to himself,
both those on the earth, and those in the heavens,
making peace through the blood of his cross.

Canticle Prayer

O God, Creator and Source of all blessings, who sent your Son, Jesus Christ, for our salvation, help us to recognize and make real the gift that daily stands before us, so that our lives may give glory to you and loving service to our brothers and sisters. Keep us alert to the magnitude of your love for each and every person, in whom you see the image of your Son, Jesus Christ, who is Lord, forever and ever.

THURSDAY

Revelation 11:17–18; 12:10b–12a

Conquest by the Blood of the Lamb

Like the previous canticle, we note that this one is also drawn from two different chapters of Revelation. In it we discover intertwined themes of reward and punishment. The canticle is preceded in the text by the account of a great earthquake (11.13), a calamity that has killed seven thousand people and brings about the fall of the city. The striking imagery of the account leads us into the message of the canticle itself: divine judgment has come upon those who were enemies of the Lord. The nations that raged against God's authority have now experienced the power of divine wrath.

The context of the canticle verses taken from chapter 12 recounts the great battle in heaven in which the archangel Michael drives out the dragon. This dragon is identified as the Devil and Satan (v. 9); those who have been faithful to God in the face of the dragon's accusations now receive redemption for their testimony to the saving acts of God. The great conquest has been accomplished by the "blood of the Lamb and the word of their witness" (v. 11). Christ's role as the great Mediator for the people of the new covenant is sealed by his blood—by his death on the cross and his resurrection. The canticle is a song of victory: God and the Lamb have conquered Satan and the forces of evil. Who are these whose love has not deterred them from death? They are the long procession of all who have offered up their lives for their faith in God and his Anointed One. This august assembly includes all who have hoped in God's promise, all who have kept this hope alive as they have looked forward to the coming of the Messiah; they are the members of the heavenly chorus who rejoice in all that God has done in bringing Christ to glory.

Revelation 11:17–18; 12:10b–12a

11:17 We give you thanks, O Lord, Almighty God,
you who are and who were.
For you have assumed your great power
and you have begun your reign.

18 The nations raged, but your wrath has come,
and the time for the dead to be judged,
and to reward your servants the prophets
and the holy ones and those who fear your name,
the small and the great alike.

12:10b Now have come the salvation
and the power and the kingdom of our God,
and the authority of his Anointed One,
for the accuser of our brethren is cast down
who accused them before our God, day and night.

11 They conquered him by the blood of the Lamb,
and by the word of their witness;
love for their life did not deter them from death.
12a Therefore, rejoice, O heavens,
and you who dwell therein.

Canticle Prayer

All powerful God, perfect in both justice and mercy: help us by your light to overcome the darkness that threatens us in the temptations of worldly power and prestige, that we may rejoice always in the victory of your Christ, who lives and reigns forever.

FRIDAY

Revelation 15:3–4

Songs of Moses and of the Lamb

This canticle is sometimes called the Song of Moses and the Song of the Lamb. In Exodus 14:31, we read, "Israel saw the great work that the LORD did against the Egyptians. So the people feared the LORD and believed in the LORD and in his servant Moses." The text then proceeds into the following chapter, comprising the great song of God's triumph known as the Canticle of Moses: this exultant paean of victory recounts the mighty deeds of God by which the threatening Egyptian army is resoundingly overcome. It asserts God's victory over the powers of both nature and human beings. Its connection to this canticle in the Book of Revelation is clear: Jesus Christ, the new Moses, has led the people of God through the trials and struggles of human life into the divine life of God. Christ is not only the new Moses; he is also the new Lamb, whose blood brings redemption to the human race. As the blood of the Passover lamb, applied to the doorposts of the Hebrew slaves, had once saved the people of God in Egypt (Exod 12:7, 12–13), now the blood of the cross brings redemption to the new people of God. The Revelation canticle links these two moments of salvation and deliverance; it speaks of them as wondrous deeds of divine righteousness.

The opening verses of the fifteenth chapter of Revelation are distinguished by three occurrences of the number seven: seven angels (15:1), seven plagues (15:5), and seven golden bowls of divine wrath (15:7). These three elements, all presented sevenfold, usher in the eschatological end-times for those who have been faithful and who are now delivered from God's wrath. Beyond chapter 15 the narrative reaches the end of the torrential overflow of God's anger. The reference to the "sea of glass" (15:2) also echoes the Exodus image of the Red Sea (or more properly "Sea of Reeds"; see especially 15:4; also cf. Exod 14:16, 15:8, and 15:10), through which the Hebrew slaves passed on foot, saved by the divine breath over the water and the power of God's right hand.

This canticle can be seen as a summary of all that God has done for the people of Israel to the present moment. Consider these great saving events: the Passover and exodus from Egypt; the second exodus from Babylon back to the promised land; and now the final Passover of Christ from death to life. What a wondrously concise statement of salvation history! It gives us an image of divine justice: God establishing a relationship with the people by means of the covenant. And though we have too often failed to uphold our end of the covenant, God always remains faithful. God stands before us as the Holy One, distinguished by mighty and wondrous works, by just and faithful deeds. To God alone belongs the glory that the whole world now beholds!

Revelation 15:3–4

3 Great and wondrous are your works,
O Lord, Almighty God!
Just and true are your ways,
O King of the nations!

4 Who would not fear, O Lord,
and glorify your name?

For you alone are the Holy One,
for all nations will come,
and they will worship before you,
for your righteous deeds have been revealed.

Canticle Prayer

God of all holiness, who by deeds of power and glory brought your people out of bondage: may we continue to grow in freedom by the blood of your Son, and so come to share in the glory that he has with you in the Spirit, forever and ever.

SEASONAL CANTICLES

EPIPHANY

1 Timothy 3:16

Christ, Taken Up in Glory

THIS CANTICLE FROM Saint Paul's First Letter to Timothy appears in the Liturgy of the Hours only twice a year: at First Vespers on the solemnity of the Epiphany, and again at Second Vespers on the Feast of the Transfiguration. Given the brevity of this one-verse text, it has been arranged to be sung as a versicle and response on both occasions, with antiphons particular to each feast.

Key words and ideas in the canticle relate to the particular feasts. "Proclaimed among the Gentiles," a reference to the so-called Three Kings—the Magi who came to worship Christ as newborn king—and "believed in throughout the world" relate to the celebration of the Epiphany, the heart of which is the universal manifestation of the Christ. The particular vocabulary of the canticle is eminently suitable to the Transfiguration, in which "flesh" and "glory" are juxtaposed; account of this event in the Gospels present Jesus in his human flesh, yet seen briefly by Peter, James, and John in brilliant light and glory, conversing with Moses and Elijah of old. Thus the words and images of this brief canticle resonate with the themes of the two feasts on which it is sung, and justify its place in the Liturgy of the Hours.

Scripture scholars have placed the First Letter of Paul to Timothy among the later writings composed in the early history of the Church, classifying it as "deutero-Pauline." This means that the text bears marked similarities to those letters whose Pauline authorship is more certain, but it clearly dates from a later period, addressing as it does issues that arose among Paul's community in the generation after his death. In the period after the death of Saint Paul and the other apostles, it sometimes happened that matters relating to their authentic teachings would be interpreted in unorthodox ways, veering from the truth and setting out on roads apart from sound doctrine. One can see in the text of 1 Timothy 4:6 and 2 Timothy 4:3 that this was an issue with which the Church was grappling. The teachings of Saint Paul were established as genuine deposits of faith (1 Tim 6:20; 2 Tim 1:12–14). It is from those authoritative instructions that these latter writings proceed to open more fully the mystery of Christ to the people and culture of the time. While the letters are pastoral and practical in establishing a particular order for the nascent Church, they also emphasize the eschatological dimension of the life of those who follow Christ. The command, "Guard what has been given you" (1 Tim 6:20) directs the followers of Christ to live in the Spirit given them in their baptism, even as they await his return in glory.

Reflecting on this short verse, one readily observes that its poetic style diverges from the standard textual form of a letter. We may take note of the contrasting images that appear in its single verse: flesh and Spirit, angels and Gentiles, the earthly world and heavenly glory. By means of these contrasting terms, the text relates its important message about Christ, the one who must always be the central focus of the matter: Jesus Christ is the God-man; he came and lived a human life on earth, visible to all, and now abides eternally in heaven. We might also consider the two credal statements found in 1 Timothy 1:15a ("This saying is trustworthy and deserves full acceptance: Christ Jesus came into the world to save sinners") and 1 Timothy 2:5–6 ("There is one God. There is also one mediator between God and the human race, Christ Jesus himself human, who gave himself as a ransom for all"). When considered with these statements, the canticle under consideration clearly contributes to the fostering of right understanding and pastoral hope in the person and teaching of Christ Jesus, in whom we have our redemption. These short verses in the midst of this letter enunciate and underscore how important it was that the Church retain its focus on Christ as it came into being and developed.

1 Timothy 3:16

℟ O praise the Lord, all you nations.

16 He was manifested in the flesh,
vindicated in the Spirit.

℟ O praise the Lord, all you nations.

He was seen by angels,
proclaimed among the Gentiles.

℟ O praise the Lord, all you nations.

He was believed in throughout the world,
taken up in glory.

℟ O praise the Lord, all you nations.

Canticle Prayer

O Christ, Lord and Savior, who in your earthly life followed perfectly the will of your Father, and so returned to the glory that was yours from the beginning: Enable us to follow you with diligence and devotion, and help us find in dedicated service to our brothers and sisters the way to peace and glory. In your holy Name we pray.

SUNDAYS IN LENT

1 Peter 2:21–24

Healed by Christ's Wounds

The Book of Isaiah includes a set of four poems known as Songs of the Servant of the Lord; they are located in Isaiah 42:1–4; 49:1–7; 50 4–9a; and 52:13—53:12. (The poems were mentioned previously in the discussion of the canticle from Philippians.) The New Testament authors, especially the evangelists, made extensive use of these poems, seeing their prophetic fulfillment in the person of Christ. The final Song of the Servant (Isa 52:13—53:12) is widely known as the Song of the Suffering Servant. This Fourth Song of the Servant is well known from its use in the liturgy; it appears as the reading at the Good Friday service. In the context of the prophet's own historical situation, many commentators identify the Servant as the nation itself: through exile and suffering, this personified figure brings about the redemption of the people. New Testament authors have associated the Suffering Servant with Jesus in various ways. Especially in this Canticle from the First Letter of Peter, the sacred author draws on the language and imagery of the Fourth Song of the Servant to show how the suffering Jesus has become a source of deliverance: his own sacrificial life has become the primary example and model of the redemptive power of suffering. The Liturgy of the Hours employs this canticle at Second Vespers on all the Sundays in Lent.

In the liturgical form of this canticle, the first part of v. 21 is not included. The omitted text reads thus: "For this you have been called, because…," from there leading directly into the canticle. The context of the passage treats the theme of patient suffering for doing what is good (v. 20). The omitted half of v. 21 serves as an important introduction to what follows, suggesting the close connection between the baptized Christian, who has been called, and Christ, who has suffered for the one thus called. The ensuing text implies that, as Jesus has done, so must his followers take on his example of patient endurance. When the canticle avers that "no guile was found on his lips" (2:22b), it echoes the Fourth Song of the Servant, where it says, "Though harshly treated, he submitted and did not open his mouth; Like a lamb led to slaughter or a sheep silent before shearers, he did not open his mouth" (Isa 53:7). We further recall that Jesus, when questioned by Pontius Pilate at his trial, remains silent (Matt 27:14; Mark 15:5). When unjustly accused and treated with contempt, Jesus remains quiet and does not defend himself. Such self-abnegation may seem difficult if not impossible in our day and age. We are taught that it is right to stand up and assert our own position. Yet often enough, silence has proven itself to be the way that ultimately allows the truth to come forth—from another's mouth, from unfolding circumstances, or from authentic eyewitnesses. One may recall the story of Susanna from the Book of Daniel: the silence of the accused woman wins her freedom (Dan 13:60–63). By his own example Jesus blesses for us a posture of silence.

When we read, "He himself bore our sins" (v. 24a), we recognize immediately the force of such a counterintuitive statement. How can anyone bear the sins of another? Should we not be obliged to take responsibility for our actions? The Fourth Servant Song inserts a radical new idea into religious thought. The text tells us: "My servant, the just one, shall justify many; their iniquity he shall bear" (53:11b). Christ, having taken our sins upon himself, was nailed to the tree. He has truly borne our sins, and being without any righteousness of our own, we are nonetheless freed from the powers of sin and death by this supreme act of love. As he "handed himself over" (1 Pet 2:23e), God accepted his offering of self, and through our union with Christ we are granted the power to die to sin and live for righteousness (24c–d). And on the basis of this model, we can see how our own suffering can be redemptive for others. Our silence is not without reason; we choose to accept suffering for a higher purpose. When we choose to unite ourselves to Christ in his suffering and silence, we can, by faith, know that our suffering may be redemptive for others.

The closing line of the canticle, "By his wounds you have been healed" (1 Pet 2:24e), is taken directly from the Fourth Servant Song: "He bore the punishment that makes us whole, by his wounds we were healed" (Isa 53:5b). This quoted assertion does not merely inspire; it serves more importantly as an appeal and summons to follow the example of Jesus. By bearing the wounds of injustice in silence and serenity, by assisting the unattractive stranger, by feeding the ungrateful panhandler, by listening to the troubled survivor of trauma, by welcoming the ungracious guest—by renouncing our own desires and bearing harsh criticisms patiently—by all these means we may take part in the healing of the Body of Christ. Wounds and abrasions come to us in manifold ways, offending our sensibilities, challenging the limits of our tolerance—and often calling for heroic patience. Responding rationally, accepting them in love, and bearing them patiently—this can be a medicinal process, a healing remedy, taken up in the name of Christ, who has first healed us.

1 Peter 2:21–24

21 Christ also suffered for you,
leaving you an example
that you should follow in his footsteps.

22 No sin did he commit;
no guile was found on his lips.

23 When he was insulted,
he returned no insult;

when he was made to suffer,
he made no threats;
instead he handed himself over
to the One who judges justly.

24 He himself bore our sins
in his own body on the tree
so that we might die to sin
and live for righteousness.
By his wounds you have been healed.

Canticle Prayer

O God, giver of all good things, we acknowledge in joy and humility that you have given us the gift of yourself in your Son Jesus, our Savior and Redeemer. Help us to know the price of our redemption, paid fully by Jesus, so that we, in turn, may follow his example by serving as ambassadors of his great mercy, who lives and reigns forever and ever.

III

GOSPEL CANTICLES

CANTICLE OF MARY (*MAGNIFICAT*)

Luke 1:46–55

Holy Is His Name

THE INFANCY NARRATIVE in the Gospel of Luke presents three canticles that we recite daily when praying the Liturgy of the Hours. Let us first consider the *Magnificat*, or Canticle of Mary. This canticle strongly resembles the Canticle of Hannah, which we find in the First Book of Samuel in the Old Testament (1:24–28). The similar language that resonates between these two canticles expresses profound joy and gratitude on the part of the two women who speak them: they give voice to jubilant gratitude for God's active participation in their lives and in the lives of their ancestors. Hannah rejoices in God's answer to her prayer: she had asked the Lord for a son, and the Lord has granted her plea; Hannah, faithful to the promise she made with her prayer, offers her son at the temple of Shiloh (1 Sam 1:20b, 24). As the Church fathers would write, Mary's joy came from first welcoming the word of God in her heart and then receiving the Son who had been promised to Israel's ancestors from of old. Both Hannah and Mary were chosen by God to receive God's loving-kindness and compassion: these women became vessels of the promise made long ago to Abraham, who was both their bodily ancestor and their father in faith.

Both of these women are presented as daughters of the household of Israel, God's chosen people, dependent upon the Lord for all things and numbered among the poor of the land. These people so dear to the Lord are often called God's *anawim*:

the poor who have no one to turn to but God alone to provide for their needs. In being unable to bear a child, Hannah felt that she lived her life under a curse. When the archangel Gabriel brought the message of the Lord to Mary, it filled her with uncertainty; all she could do was wait for God's word to be fulfilled according to the divine will. The situations of both Hanna and Mary may be understood as anxious waiting upon God; placing their faith in God, they persevered in allowing the divine plan to unfold in their lives. Luke's infancy narrative presents Elizabeth and Zechariah, like Mary, as *anawim*: faithful servants of God who wait upon the divine will. The infancy narrative of Matthew does the same for Joseph, the righteous man who faithfully and obediently serves God in his care for Mary and Jesus.

When we look closely at the text of the passage in which we find Mary's canticle, we may be surprised by a specific turn of phrase in the translated text: "and she said." Elizabeth had been speaking immediately prior to the appearance of this phrase. Who are we to understand has proclaimed the canticle? Does the pronoun *she* indeed refer to Mary, as has been traditionally assumed—or to Elizabeth, who had just welcomed Mary to her home? The strongest early traditions of the Latin translations attribute the canticle to Mary, and the passage has been thus understood through the centuries. The sequence of the narrative, then, presents Elizabeth's praise of her relative Mary, who then responds with her proclamation of the wonders that God has accomplished in her, wonders that fulfill through her the promise made to Abraham (v. 55), and anticipate that all generation will indeed refer to her as blessed (v. 48), as her cousin Elizabeth has herself just done.

On one occasion, when the crowd following Jesus tells him that his mother and his brothers wish to see him, Jesus replies, "My mother and my brothers are those who hear the word of God and act on it" (Luke 8:21; cf. also Mark 3:33–35). Mary is of course the perfect model of one who hears the word of God and acts on it; for this reason she is often called the first of Christ's disciples. When we understand this about Mary, we attain a deeper appreciation for her words in the *Magnificat*. She rejoices in the word of God in her heart and its accomplishment in her life. Several elements in the canticle resonate with the idea of Mary as the first disciple. Mary's insight into her own lowliness places her among those who had been the *anawim* of the Old Testament, so dearly beloved by God. She acknowledges a firsthand experience of God's wondrous power—God is doing great things for her: she has a special insight and experience of divine mercy. The teaching of Luke's Gospel emphasizes a love of the poor (Luke 4:18; 6:20; 7:22; 18:22; 21:2–3); it is in this context that Mary refers to herself as one of God's lowly ones.

In v. 49b of the canticle, Mary proclaims of God, "Holy is his name." What is the significance of this line? Holiness in the Scriptures designates a state of being set apart, as belonging to God. Furthermore, the scriptural authors understood the "name" of someone as both capturing and expressing their unique character, their identity—their personal power. In this case, God's very identity and holiness have touched the life of Mary with both power and goodness—power that prepares her for a unique mission; goodness that cares for her with the love and mercy she has experienced, recognized, and acknowledged. Again, Mary knows her own place among the *anawim*—those Old Testament figures who experienced the favor and care of God despite the lowliness of their own being and circumstances. The prophet Isaiah expresses profoundly the great mystery of divine love for these people: God is "the One who dwells forever, whose name is holy: I dwell in a high and holy place, but also with the contrite and lowly of spirit, to revive the spirit of the lowly, to revive the heart of the crushed" (57:15). Mary finds her identity as one of God's little ones, sustained by the overwhelming goodness that God shows toward her.

The posture of waiting is a very holy attitude to adopt. It moves us to put our total trust in what God alone can bring to fruition, forming in us a faith-filled hope. As God unfolds the plans of our lives, if we see with faith we come to understand that we are part of the divine plan, something much bigger than ourselves or our own designs. As it came to be for both Hannah and the Virgin Mary, God's life plan is more fruitful than we could have achieved or imagined by ourselves. Thus each of us is able to acclaim our own *Magnificat*, to tell of God's wonders at work in our lives. Living in the assurance of God's grace at work within us, our lives are enriched, and we are able to become ambassadors to others of the divine plan that informs their own lives.

Luke 1:46–55

46 My soul proclaims the greatness of the Lord,
47 and my spirit rejoices in God my Savior,
48 for he has looked upon his handmaid in her lowliness;
for behold, from this day forward,
all generations will call me blessed.

49 For the Almighty has done great things for me,
and holy is his name.
50 His mercy is from age to age
for those who fear him.

51 He has made known the strength of his arm,
and has scattered the proud in their conceit of heart.
52 He has cast down the mighty from their thrones
and has exalted those who are lowly.
53 He has filled the hungry with good things,
and has sent the rich away empty.

54 He has helped his servant Israel,
mindful of his mercy,

[55] even as he promised to our fathers,
to Abraham and his descendants forever.

Canticle Prayer

God of our salvation, help us to discern in the canticle of the Virgin Mary a proclamation of your wondrous care and guidance for your people. Grant us the vision to see your loving hand at work in our lives, in our world, and in your Church. Grant that we too might proclaim our own song of praise with hearts full of gratitude and thanksgiving. May we always bear witness to your love in our lives, through Christ our Lord.

CANTICLE OF ZECHARIAH (*BENEDICTUS*)

Luke 1:68–79

The Tender Mercy of God

Let us first note that the Canticle of Zechariah concludes with the phrase "to guide our feet into the way of peace." The word *peace* appears a dozen times in the Gospel of Luke, more than in any of the other Gospels. It is an important theme for this evangelist. When we think of peace today, it brings to mind an absence of anxiety, a sense of serenity and tranquility. While this is not far from the biblical notion of peace, the biblical mind understood the word to contain something more. An understanding of wholeness accompanies the biblical notion of peace—totality and unity of well-being, good health, tranquility of heart, freedom from danger. The first appearance of *peace* in the Lucan Gospel occurs at the nativity of Jesus, where the angels announce, "Glory to God in the highest and on earth peace to those on whom his favor rests" (Luke 2:14). The Messiah comes to usher in an era of peace that, according to the Gospel, will bring blessing and prosperity to all. We plead for this each day as we pray the Canticle of Zechariah.

Verse 75 presents a text that we may overlook simply because we recite it daily. Yet it is an important passage that speaks to a significant form of growth and development in our lives. The text speaks of a state in which we are "freed from the hands of our foes," and "may serve [God] *without fear*, in *holiness* and righteousness, all the days of our life." One of the most frequent expressions of Jesus in the Gospels is "Do not fear." Here the Canticle of Zechariah speaks of the only way to attain freedom from fear—the unique way in which *holiness* is found on this our path of life: that is, by following and holding fast to the teaching of Jesus and by imitating his example. While this course may sound broad and lofty, even perhaps a little vague—all we have to do is look deep within ourselves and our heart will reveal to us where we are on the path to *holiness*. Holiness is a passage through the paschal mystery, beset with struggle and uncertainty, and even pain and sadness. Yet true holiness encourages us to set our fears aside. We can be assured of holiness if we enter and persevere on the path of the paschal mystery; it will lead us to its proper and inevitable end—which is nothing short of the glory of God.

The context in which the Canticle of Zechariah appears reminds us that John's birth, like those of certain figures from the Old Testament, manifests God's presence and design in the unfolding of salvation. God brings forth particular individuals in unique situations to take up a special mission in service to the divine purpose: Sarah, Abraham's wife, who gave birth to Isaac (Gen 11); the prophet Samuel, who was born from a mother who had been unable to give birth (1 Sam 1); and Samson, whose narrative presents his mysterious birth as foretold by a mysterious messenger (Judg 13).

In a narrative style recalling these illustrious predecessors, John the Baptist appears as the prophet of the Most High, prophet of the new age of salvation, prophet of the new and eternal covenant—the last of the great prophets of Israel. John ushers in the age where the covenant blessing is revealed as a kingdom of grace that promises forgiveness from sin. Jeremiah had foretold this coming age as a time when "everyone, from the least to the greatest shall know [God]…for [God] will forgive their iniquity and no longer remember their sin" (31:34). The Psalmist puts it much the same way: "[God] does not treat us according to our sins, nor repay us according to our faults. As far as the east is from the west, so far from us does he remove our transgression" (Ps 103:10, 12). And Malachi prophesies the coming Messiah as "the sun of justice [who] will arise with healing in his wings" (3:20). John is the one who will prepare the way for the Messiah: "I am baptizing you with water for repentance, but the one who is coming after me is mightier than I" (Matt 3:11). And his clarion call is eschatological: "Repent, for the kingdom of heaven is at hand!" (Matt 3:2).

As Israel has known for centuries, the House of David is the chosen vessel from which God shall bring forth the Messiah (2 Samuel 7). And yet the story of David was clearly presented in constantly opposing sensibilities: blessing and punishment, forthrightness and intrigue, furtiveness and force, election and rejection, wisdom and folly, love and hate. Yet through all of these cycles of David's triumphs and failures, God remains faithful to his House. The prophets are often called to confront the repeated breakings of the covenant by the people among whom they live. Conversion and repentance, exile and deliverance, become both their message and their pattern of life. God continues to call them back with the renewed promise of grace. Abraham, the father of their faith, receives the unlikely invitation to start life over again at an advanced age. His own faith is tested in the promise of a son through his sterile wife; he is obedient even when the promise appears to be on the point of retraction; and he is finally liberated by God's intervening word. The fidelity of Abraham is constantly reiterated for Israel through the texts of Scripture as a pattern that the always faithful God puts before his servants.

The Canticle of Zechariah announces both the history of deliverance and the dawn of the new and definitive salvation. The Old Testament figures that appear in this canticle are not chronologically presented, but they nonetheless recall the story of God's plan: they are key characters whose individual stories comprise the glorious and mysterious history of divine grace. The House of David, the prophets, father Abraham—and finally John the Baptist, the prophet who announces the dawn of salvation. All of these figures have experienced a personal call from God that, when accepted, suspends them in dramatic narrative tension, as their lives both clarify and conceal the One whose tender mercies lead us all forward from darkness to light. The mystery of God's relationship with the human race always guides us, as it guided them, to new heights of service, self-surrender, and overflowing grace.

Luke 1:68–79

68 Blessed be the Lord God of Israel:
for he has visited his people and redeemed them;
69 he has raised up for us a horn of salvation
in the House of David his servant,
70 as he spoke through the mouth of his holy ones,
his prophets from ages past:

71 to grant salvation from our foes,
and from the hand of all who hate us,
72 showing mercy to our fathers,
remembering his holy covenant,
73 the oath he swore to Abraham our father;

74 to grant that, freed from the hand of our foes,
75 we may serve him without fear

in holiness and righteousness
all the days of our life.

[76] And you, little child, will be called
the Prophet of the Most High,
for you will go before the Lord
to make ready his ways:
[77] to grant knowledge of salvation to his people
by the forgiveness of their sins;

[78] through the tender mercy of our God,
the Dawn from on high will visit us,
[79] to shine on those who sit in darkness,
and those in the shadow of death;
to guide our feet into the way of peace.

Canticle Prayer

O God of the Covenant, lead us to discover in your tender mercy toward us the peace that is your will for our world. Amid the challenges that we must face, help us to know your mysterious plan for our salvation even as it unfolds in our lives. Instill in us the trust that will draw us forward, finding your gracious care for us in each passing day. Through Christ our Lord.

CANTICLE OF SIMEON (*NUNC DIMITTIS*)

Luke 2:29–32

A Light to the Nations

Artistic portrayals of this scene from Luke's Gospel often depict Simeon and Anna as elderly patrons of the temple. Looking upon their faces, one can see that they are nearing the end of their life's journey, and are grateful for this wonderful encounter with the infant Jesus and his human parents. The two elders are clothed in the garments of the temple guardians, something akin to the formal custodians of present-day churches. And while those images may certainly help to form our understanding of the scene, the meaning of the Greek text is more nuanced than the art is able to portray. We read Simeon's words, "Now you dismiss your servant in peace" (v. 29). The most obvious meaning is that Simeon, having beheld the baby who will become Israel's savior, is now ready for death. But there is more to Simeon's response than this. The sense of his words includes the notion that by this encounter, Simeon is finally released from a specific task or responsibility that God had in fact commissioned him to carry out. By the power and work of the Holy Spirit, Simeon was able to see and hold in his arms the One who would come to be recognized as the Messiah of the Lord: having lived his long life as a just and righteous man, Simeon had become worthy of this extraordinary honor. He had taken on the work of maintaining this stature before God and had thus come to merit the privilege of personally encountering the long-awaited Messiah. Three times the text tells us that the Holy Spirit was with Simeon, guiding and blessing him. He had patiently "await[ed] the consolation of Israel" having been told by the Spirit "that he should not see death before he had seen the Messiah of the Lord" (Luke 2:25–26). By faith he knew that the Holy Spirit would move him to fulfill this privileged duty. In our own lives, the Holy Spirit, given us at our baptism, is forever prompting us in the ways of the Lord's will for goodness, insight, charity, peace, and service. May we be attentive to these gentle and holy promptings in our own lives!

There are times in our life when we, too, carry a charge or obligation. In such times we may be guided by a movement from within our hearts to do good, to perform justice, to show compassion—to follow the promptings of the Spirit speaking in our hearts. We see Simeon as one touched by the Holy Spirit through his righteous living; he has led a life of longing for the fulfillment of God's promised new age of redemption and deliverance. His words bear a prophetic quality in the Gospel of Luke. In this evangelist's account of the birth of Jesus, a multitude of the heavenly host has proclaimed, "Glory to God in the highest and on earth peace to those on whom his favor rests" (2:14). Now Simeon proclaims that this child is to be "a light of revelation to the nations, and the glory of your people Israel" (2:32). Luke's narrative expands the gift of God's peace announced with the birth of Jesus to include the Gentile world, for whom he will be a "light," guiding all who follow his word, as Zechariah had declared in his own canticle, "into the way of peace" (1:79). The Lucan Gospel presents Jesus as continually opening himself and his mission to the Gentile world, affirming that the salvation of God is open to all people who believe and find consolation in the Gospel's message. Luke's message is sometimes referred to as the universal call to salvation, God's invitation to redemption open to all people of all times.

We see, then, how the word *peace* appears at critical points in the infancy narrative of the Gospel of Luke: in the announcement by the angels of the peace that accompanies the birth of Jesus; in the Canticle of Zechariah, where we are guided in the way of peace; and now in the Canticle of Simeon, where the faithful old man accepts the peace that comes with his completed mission. In these canticles Luke reiterated his theme of peace at a time when the hope for peace in a world under the domination of the Roman Empire was in serious doubt. The people of Israel at that time were forced to endure external control of their land, the imposition of taxes that diminished their prosperity, tensions generated by cultural prejudice, the threat of oppressive war, and conflict with the religious beliefs of their overlords that undermined their own internal cohesion. Israel's persistent hope for *peace*, interwoven with the promise of the coming Messiah, became ultimately the gateway through which Christianity emerged into the ancient world. The great expectation and promise of the prophets had anticipated the eventual establishment of peaceful coexistence among all peoples and cultures; such peace would usher in the Messianic era. And this longing for worldwide peace remains our enduring hope today. We look for peace in so many areas of our lives, realizing that it can only be a gift of God, something for which we must fervently pray. We do well to remember the tag from a familiar song, "Let Peace Begin with Me." Though the words are simple, even perhaps a little trite, they remain none-theless a daily invitation to make simple adjustments to our own little corners of the world—to strive in our own lives to be loving and compassionate, to accept the peace that is God's gracious gift. Thousands of years ago, the Psalmist put into perfect words the longing of our own hearts: "Let us hear what the LORD God speaks; he speaks of peace for his people and his faithful, and those who turn their hearts to him" (Ps 85:9). Let it be so!

Luke 2:29–32

29 Now you dismiss your servant in peace,
according to your word, O Master;

30 for my eyes have seen your salvation,
31 which you prepared in the sight of all the peoples:

32 a light for revelation to the nations,
and the glory of your people Israel.

Canticle Prayer

O Maker of the universe, who bring forth the dawn and draw day to its close, help us to recall with gratitude the blessings of this day, even with its failings and regrets, knowing that tomorrow you will offer us a new day in which we may reaffirm our dedication to you as the source of our strength and courage. And when we come to the twilight of life, may we readily offer back to you all the days you have given us, with the sure hope in your gracious redemption, through Christ our Lord.